THE OAKLAND–SAN FRANCISCO BAY BRIDGE TROLL

THE OAKLAND–SAN FRANCISCO BAY BRIDGE TROLL

JOHN V. ROBINSON

AMERICA
THROUGH TIME®
ADDING COLOR TO AMERICAN HISTORY

For Maryam Rezapour, who accompanied me around the Bay Area interviewing people and taking photographs. It is to Maryam that this book is affectionately dedicated.

America Through Time is an imprint of Fonthill Media LLC
www.through-time.com
office@through-time.com

Published by Arcadia Publishing by arrangement with Fonthill Media LLC
For all general information, please contact Arcadia Publishing:
Telephone: 843-853-2070
Fax: 843-853-0044
E-mail: sales@arcadiapublishing.com
For customer service and orders:
Toll-Free 1-888-313-2665

www.arcadiapublishing.com

First published 2018

ISBN 978-1-63499-044-8

Typeset in Minion Pro 11pt on 17pt
Printed and bound by CPI Group (UK) Ltd, Croydon CR0 4YY

CONTENTS

A NOTE ON THE INTERVIEWS

I have in the past interviewed various people about their experiences with my topics. Most notably, Al Zampa, the legendary bridgeman who worked on the Bay Bridge and the Golden Gate Bridge in the 1930s. In such cases I quote from their interviews extensively to give them a voice in the story I am recounting. See, for example, *Bay Area Iron Master Al Zampa* (2017). The same is true in this book. I have allowed each person interviewed to tell their story in their own words. I have edited the interviews for continuity, and quietly edited out repetitions, unrelated asides, and false starts. I have not interjected any of my own opinions into the interviews.

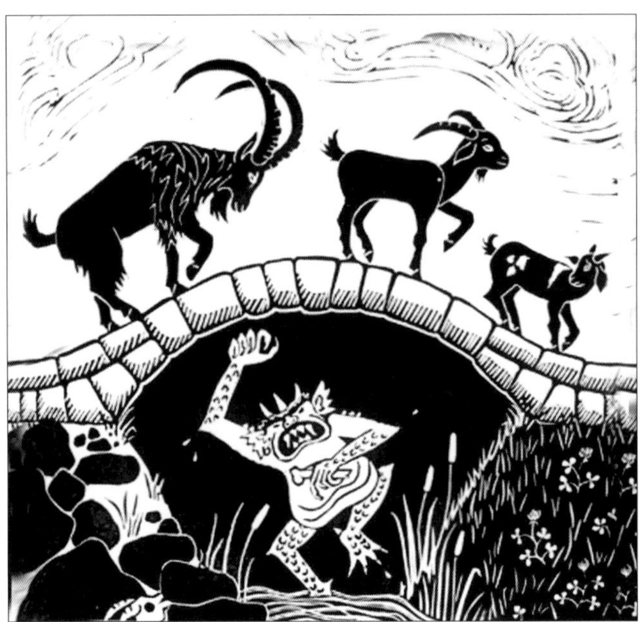

This classic rendition of the popular children's tale, *Three Billy Goats Gruff*, shows a threatening troll under a bridge with the three goats crossing above. This story is why many people today associate trolls with bridges. I like this image because it has similar gargoyle features as Bill Roan's 1989 troll. Bill Roan, for his part, states that he thought of the *Three Billy Goats Gruff* story as inspiration for his troll. (Image by Anne E.G. Nydam, 2006. nydamprints.com.)

ACKNOWLEDGEMENTS

I have spent twenty-five years monitoring the Bay Bridge Troll and over those years many people have shared my interest in this mysterious statute. My academic friends and mentors, Archie Green (1917-2009) and Alan Dundes (1934-2005), were chief among them. I knew about the troll for several years before I started my undergraduate work at UC Berkeley. But, it was only after taking Alan Dundes' popular folklore course that I understood the significance of the little troll. It was Alan Dundes who suggested I get in touch with Archie Green, a labor historian and folklorist. Archie Green, too, appreciated the troll's significance to Bay Area history and lore and encouraged my investigation of the troll and other aspects of laborlore associated with bridges and iron workers.

I am also indebted to Bill Roan, the troll's creator, for sharing his recollections about the troll and musing on its place in the popular imagination and history of the Bay Area's bridges. Likewise, Michael Bondi, of Michael Bondi Metal Designs in Richmond, California, shared his memories about both the old and new trolls that were created, in 1989 and 2013, in his shop. Bondi graciously shared photographs of both the old and new trolls.

Special thanks go to James "Fish" Sturgeon, and his wife, Jeanette, who welcomed me and Maryam into their Vacaville home where I talked with Jim Sturgeon and Brett Clark about their work on the new bridge and listened to

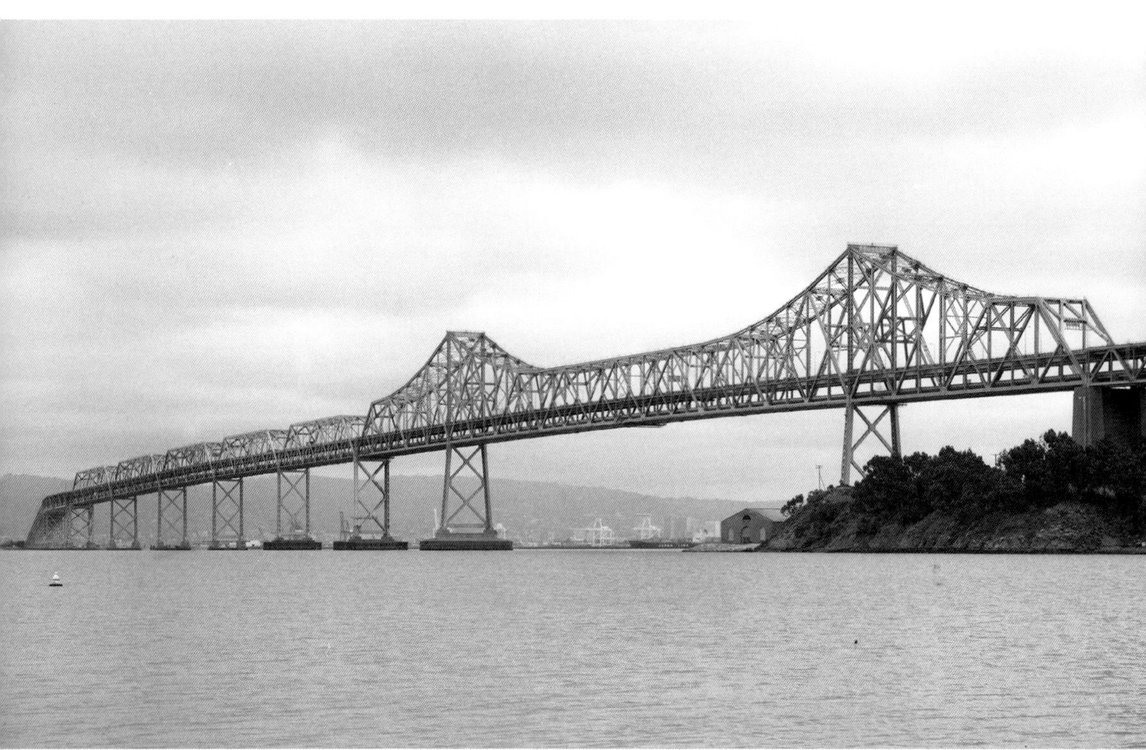

The eastern span of the Oakland San Francisco Bay Bridge, shown here in 1999, was badly damaged in the 1989 Loma Prieta Earthquake. The Bay Bridge Troll was installed to the repaired section. Not long after this photo was taken, construction was started on the replacement span. As I write this, the new span is open, and the old span is completely gone. (Courtesy of the Library of Congress.)

Jim's story about the attempt to "liberate" the troll when the old span was closed to traffic in August 2013. "Fish" was also in the unique position of handling the new troll before it was installed on the new bridge a few months later, thereby making Jim Sturgeon one of the very few people to put hands on both the old and the new Bay Bridge Trolls.

Amiee Brooks, Matt Janulewicz, and Tom Meyers all made welcome contributions to my understanding of the troll's penetration into pop culture. Lindsay Wright, at the Oakland Museum, provided photos of the troll's appearance at the Bay Bridge exhibit in 2013. Thank you also to Donald Zampa, at the District

Council of Iron Workers of the State of California and Vicinity, for putting me in touch with James Sturgeon. (It's good to have friends in high places.)

I have made an honest attempt to locate the photographers and give them credit for their work. When I could not find out who took the photographs, I credit the people who shared them with me. Thanks, as well, to Jeff Rubin for inviting me to talk to the Pinole Historical Society about the Bay Bridge Troll, giving me a forum to publicly talk about the troll and receive audience feedback, which helped me organize my thoughts on this subject.

All these people shared their stories, their art, and their photographs with me. But most importantly they shared my interest in this unusual and little-known icon of San Francisco Bay Area culture. Thank you one and all.

John V. Robinson
August 2017

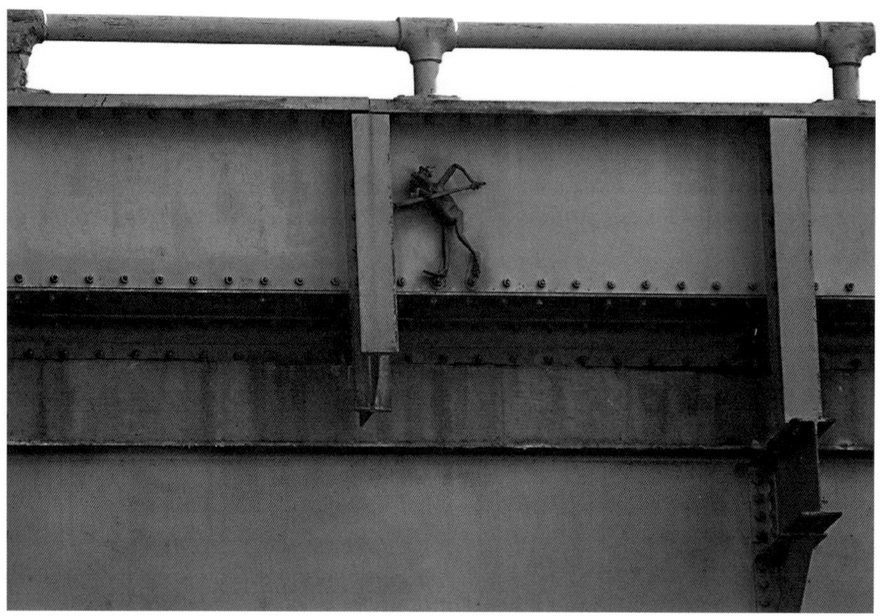

Troll at his duty station on the Bay Bridge. (Author's files.)

INTRODUCTION

I have long been aware of, and interested in, the little metal sculpture that was attached to the eastern-span old Bay Bridge (demolished in 2017) and known popularly as the "Bay Bridge Troll." Being aware of the little troll, but unsure of its significance to Bay Area history and bridge lore, I had mentioned it in various publications to remind people of its existence and point the way for future interested parties. In 2001, I published an article in the journal *Western Folklore* on the iron workers' custom of "topping out." I used the Bay Bridge Troll as an example of a topping out custom adopted to an unusual circumstance. I included a photograph of the troll, provided by the California Department of Transportation (Caltrans), taken that day in 1989 the little troll was placed on the bridge.

A few years later, in 2005, I did a small book for Arcadia Publishing, titled *Al Zampa and the Bay Area Bridges*. In that book I included a chapter on the old Bay Bridge, with brief remarks and early photographs of the new bridge's construction. Here again, I published a photograph of the troll and mentioned the circumstances of its creation. By that time the long-promised replacement span was under construction, but still many years from completion. Even at that late date, I hadn't given much thought to what might become of the Bay Bridge Troll when the new bridge opened. On some level, I secretly hoped some band of rogue iron workers would "liberate" the troll and it would disappear into history and legend. (I must confess that some of those imagined scenarios ended with me in possession of the troll.)

When the new Bay Bridge was nearing completion in 2013, I knew something would become of the little troll, but what? There were discussions about the troll in the media and on various online forums (there was, for a time, a "Save the Bay Bridge Troll" Facebook page): Should the troll be removed and placed on the new bridge? Should the new bridge have a new troll? How would that happen? Officially? Or would the new bridge get a new troll in the same unofficial way the old bridge got its troll, i.e., guerilla-art tactics?

Not surprisingly, there were vocal advocates supporting the various possibilities. Some called for a formal ceremony to retire the old troll, others hoped for the intervention of bridge workers to liberate the old troll and have it "appear" on the new bridge without ceremony, warning, or invitation. Caltrans could not openly support that chaotic plan, but I suspect they would not have tried too hard to foil such an attempt and accepted the situation with a wink and nod.

As it turns out, all of the above happened to one degree or another: iron workers went onto the old bridge just moments after it was forever closed to traffic and began removing the old troll, police were called, and there was a scene. The old troll was claimed by bridge officials and trotted out in a makeshift retirement ceremony held at the old paint-warehouse near the entrance to the pedestrian and bike path onto the new bridge. A new troll was made and placed on the new bridge with little fanfare and possibly without Caltrans' knowledge or approval.

I think it might help, at this point, to clarify some details for readers that do not live in the San Francisco Bay Area. The eastern span of the Oakland-San Francisco Bay Bridge consists of a cantilever bridge that connects Oakland with Yerba Buena Island in the middle of the bay. A tunnel leads traffic through the island onto two suspension bridges laid end to end on the western, San Francisco, side of the tunnel. The entire structure is eight miles long. The eastern span between Oakland and Yerba Buena was damaged by the 1989 earthquake. That section of the bridge was replaced by the new span. (The picture on the front cover of this book is of the new replacement of the eastern span.) The eastern span of the old bridge was then demolished.

In the decade before the new Bay Bridge's 2013 opening I had done several large photography and writing projects documenting the many interesting, but lesser known, bridges of the San Francisco Bay Area. The new Bay Bridge was the last of a decade long building spree that gave the Bay Area a second generation of great bridges. My interest in these new bridges led to the publication of several books, including: *Spanning the Strait: Building the Alfred Zampa Memorial Bridge* (2004), *Building the Benicia-Martinez Bridge* (2007), and *Carquinez Bridge 1927-2007* (2017). So, over the course of those years, I became knowledgeable about the cultural history of the Bay Area's bridges.

My interest in our local bridges, the deconstruction of the eastern span of old Bay Bridge, and my knowledge of the Bay Bridge Troll made the timing of a book seem right. My goal in this book is to get everybody on the record with their best recollections of the creation, installation, and removal of the original 1989 Bay Bridge Troll. Then I expand the subject to include the creation and installation of the new troll, unofficially known as "Junior."

Now that the old bridge is gone, and the old troll is retired from active service, I thought it important to sort out the truth from the legend and find out where the Bay Bridge Troll is, as of this publication, and what might become of it in the future.

Over the past several years a lot of rumors and misconceptions have circulated regarding the Bay Bridge Troll. Some of that is to be expected, and indeed is good, as it is part of the little troll's ascension to that of a Bay Area legend. Currently the Bay Bridge Troll has a Wikipedia page, a Facebook page, and a little-known twin—also created by Bill Roan for the contractor, Rigging International, who repaired the quake damaged Bay Bridge in 1989. With so many rumors and questions swirling around the Bay Bridge Troll, I thought the time was right to sort out the story. I talked to many of the people involved with the various trolls to record their thoughts and recollections on the trolls' creation, nearly twenty-five years of obscure toil on the old bridge, as well as the people involved with the old troll's removal and the creation and installation of the new troll.

So, here is the story, as best I can piece together, of the Bay Bridge Troll, its twin, its younger sibling (Junior) and the many people who have worked to create the legend of the Oakland-San Francisco Bay Bridge Troll.

1

OCTOBER 17, 1989, 5:04 P.M.

At 5 p.m. Pacific time, ABC Sports went on the air with the pregame show for Game 3 of the 1989 World Series between the two Bay Area teams, the San Francisco Giants and the Oakland A's. The entire Bay Area was caught up in the World Series excitement. Famously, the great quake occurred on live TV as sportscaster Al Michaels and Tim McCarver were delivering the pregame introductions to the television audience. About four minutes into the broadcast, the TV picture went blank and Al Michaels could be heard saying, "I tell you what … we are having an earthq … " The screen went blank for a few seconds before an ABC World Series logo reappeared on the screens around the country and television viewers began to hear Al Michaels' static voice, "Well, heh, I don't know if we are on the air … we are in commercial … I guess." After a few seconds of confusion, the broadcast team regained their composure and Michaels announced, "Well, folks, that's the greatest open in the history of television. Bar none."

That is how the rest of the country learned that a devastating 6.9 earthquake had struck the San Francisco Bay Area. Known to history as the Loma Prieta earthquake (named for an obscure mountain at the quake's epicenter near Santa Cruz).

In October of 1989, I was working as an iron worker. The Iron Workers Oakland Local 378 union hall was on Campbell St. in West Oakland, one block west of the devastated Cypress Freeway. The images of the damaged bridge

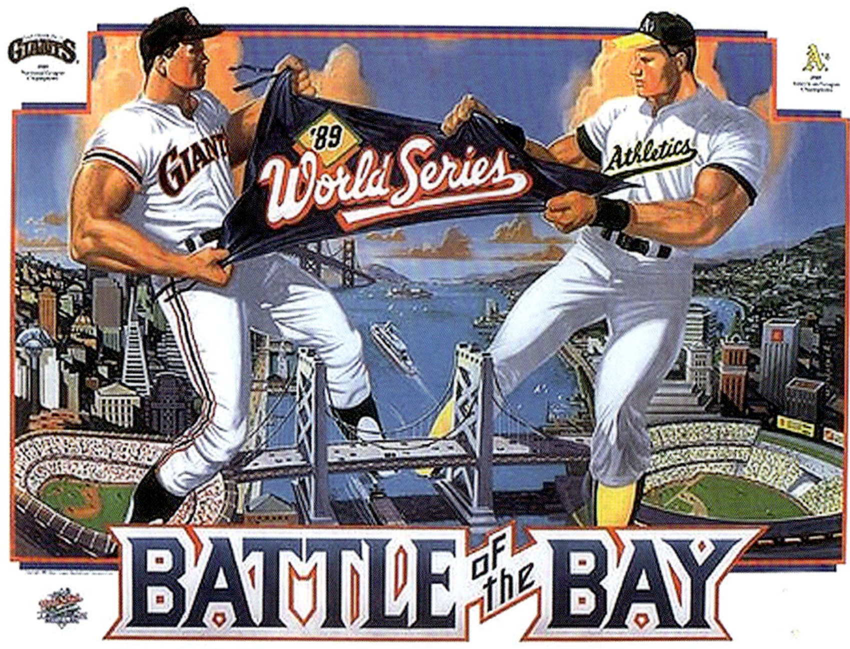

In 1989 the Oakland A's and the San Francisco Giants faced off in the 1989 World Series. The series was known locally as the Bay Bridge Series. Here, a poster depicts two opposing ball players astride the suspension span of the Bay Bridge connecting Candlestick Park with the Oakland Coliseum. The earthquake changed all that and the series became known, from game three on, as the "Earthquake Series." The A's defeated the Giants four games to none, despite the earthquake's interruption. (Author's collection.)

and the burning and collapsed buildings of San Francisco's Marina District got more media attention, but Cypress Freeway was where many people died when the upper deck of the freeway pancaked onto the lower deck, and in some places, further down to the ground. The following morning the iron workers and other building trades answered the call to stabilize the structure and begin the grim process of body recovery. A total of sixty-three people lost their lives during the quake. But most, forty-two of those people, died sitting in their cars, on the one-and-a-quarter-mile section of the Cypress Freeway that pierced west Oakland leading to the Bay Bridge. The death toll would have been higher, but traffic was light that day as many people had left work early

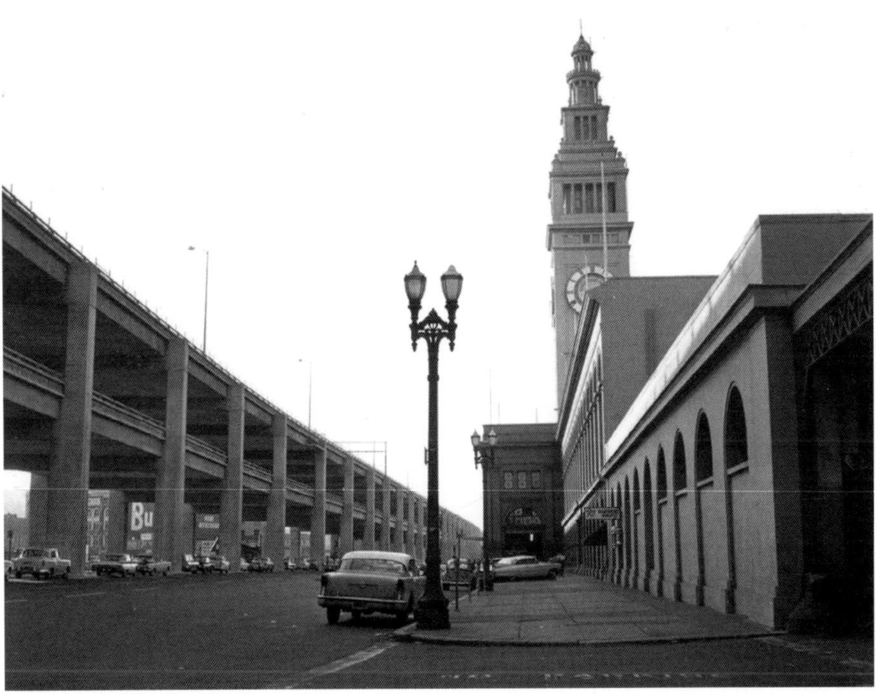

This view from the early 1960s shows the double-deck Embarcadero Freeway looking north near the Ferry Building. It gives some idea as to what the Cypress Freeway looked like before it collapsed in 1989. Though not badly damaged in the earthquake, the Embarcadero was red-tagged, along with the Central Freeway, and demolished in the 1990s. The beautiful open space along the Embarcadero today is due to the Loma Prieta Earthquake. (Author's collection.)

to watch Game 3 of the 1989 World Series. For that reason, the 1989 quake is locally referred to as the "World Series earthquake."

The collapse, demolition, and removal of the Cypress Freeway didn't just affect Oakland, but it drastically changed and improved the San Francisco skyline as well. Before the earthquake, traffic moved into downtown San Francisco on the double deck Embarcadero Freeway—an ugly and intrusive structure that ran like a wall in front of the iconic Ferry Building, separating the downtown from the waterfront for the expedient of dumping traffic onto Broadway.

The original plan was to extend the Embarcadero Freeway all the way to the Golden Gate Bridge. The 1966 "Freeway Revolt," where people rallied against these intrusions into their neighborhoods, put an end to any future freeway expansions. This revolt included the double-decked Central Freeway, which gouged a path through the Hayes Valley and Western Addition neighborhoods, and which was also closed and tagged for demolition after the 1989 earthquake. It's hard to imagine a time when urban planners thought adding these double-decked eyesores was an improvement to San Francisco. The earthquake of 1989, and the collapse of the Nimitz Freeway in Oakland, is the main reason these freeways were red-tagged and torn down in San Francisco.

On that fateful October day, I left work at 3:30 and hurried home to watch third game of the World Series. I came up interstate 880 and passed through (for the last time) the double-decked section of the freeway in Oakland, known as the Cyprus Freeway, near where Interstates 580, 880, and 80 converge at the Bay Bridge to funnel commuters in and out of San Francisco.

At 5:00 p.m. I was standing in the living room of my Crockett apartment. My T.V. was tuned to local ABC affiliate Channel 7. Al Michaels and Tim McCarver were recounting the first two games, won by the Oakland A's, in Oakland. At 5:04 p.m. the picture on my screen glitched out and I thought I heard Al Michaels say, "I'll tell you what, we're having an earthq … " It took a few seconds for the seismic waves to roll the twenty miles north to Crockett where I was listening to the T.V. Just as Michaels' words registered in my mind, the building undulated, I heard people gasp and yell a bit, and I struggled to keep my balance for a brief second. Oddly, my first thought was not earthquake, but rowdy neighbors celebrating the start of the game. Then it was over. I had felt several minor tremors in my life, but this was different. It seemed more substantial. I realized the severity of the jolt when all the local San Francisco television stations were knocked off the air.

It took some minutes for the various San Francisco-based channels to regroup and begin broadcasting again. Because of the World Series broadcast, ABC News was in the best position to covet the event nationally. They had satellite trucks linked to all the ABC affiliates around the country. They also had the

Goodyear Blimp in the air above the game to give a bird's eye view to television viewers around the country.

Here in the Bay Area, ABC Channel 7 was crippled for several hours and had a very hard time reporting to us what was happening. I switched around to different channels to see what was happening. The quake, which was centered in Santa Cruz about fifty miles south of San Francisco, is said to have released the energy of thirty Hiroshima bombs. (Who calculates these things and why they use Hiroshima as a base line, I do not know.) However you reckon it, the quake flattened the city of Santa Cruz, destroying over 700 homes and 300 businesses. Thousands more were damaged to varying degrees. People who visit downtown Santa Cruz today see beautiful modern buildings. The earthquake obliterated the older buildings downtown and the rebuilt city today is the effect of the great quake of 1989.

The waves created by the fault's slippage moved in all directions like the ripples on a still pond after a stone is cast into it. To the west was the Pacific Ocean, to the east was sparsely populated agricultural communities, and to the south were smaller cities of Watsonville and Monterey, with Watsonville bearing the brunt of the damage. But sixty miles to the north were more densely populated cites of the Bay Area where the wrath of quake would be felt the most severely.

During the weeks after the quake, I, like many other construction workers, was dispatched to several locations around the East Bay to help in the cleanup and recovery efforts. Several times I was called to the collapsed section of the Cyprus Freeway to assist in stabilizing sections that hadn't completely collapsed and begin removing the tons of rubble, as well as the stranded and mangled cars from the scene. For most of its length the top deck pancaked down on top of the lower deck. In a few sections, the top and bottom decks fell to the ground, bringing many tons of concrete and steel down to the surface streets. Hundreds of cars were damaged, and dozens of people were killed. During one of my shifts, I brought a cheap Polaroid camera with me and captured a few snap shots of the shocking destruction. (I hadn't yet discovered my interest in construction photography that would come to define the early 2000s for me. But the impulse was already with me.)

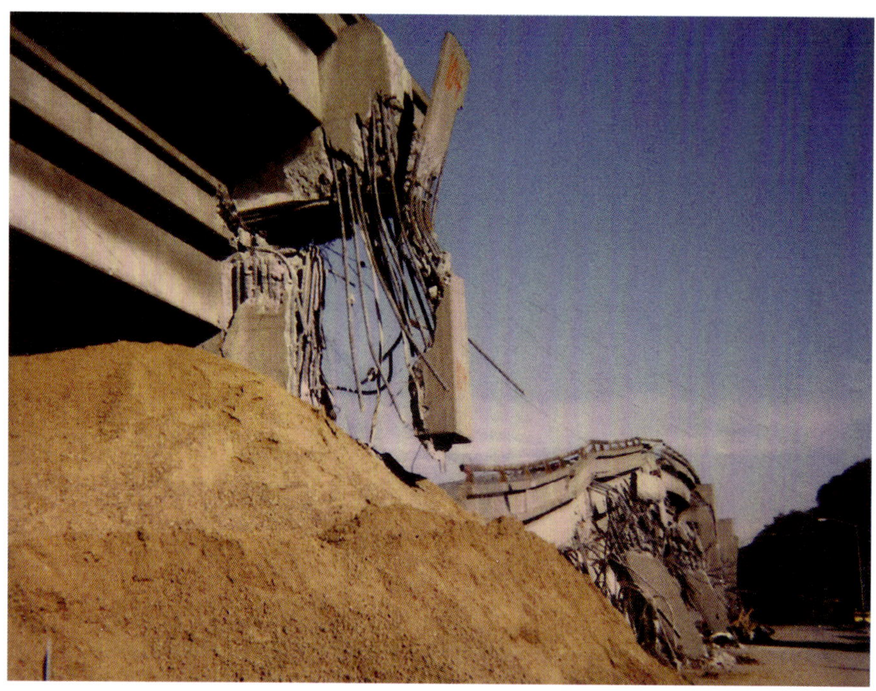

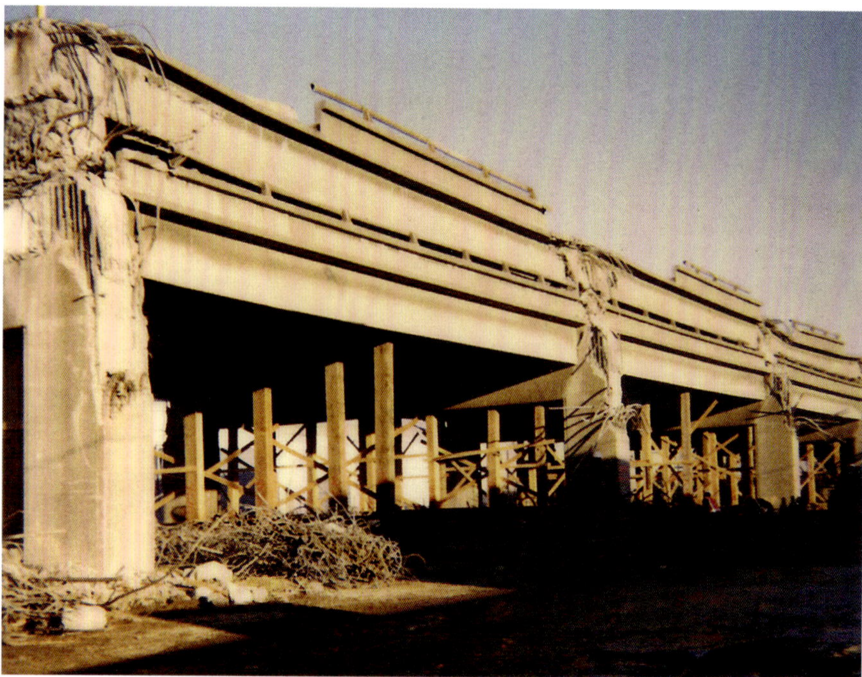

In October of 1989, I was working as an iron worker. Like many of my fellow iron workers I was called down to the collapsed Cypress Freeway in Oakland. On one occasion, I brought a cheap Polaroid camera and took a few snapshots of the damage. The two photos here show the sand used to stabilize parts of the fallen structure and the wooden supports used to keep other sections from further collapse. (Photographs by John V. Robinson.)

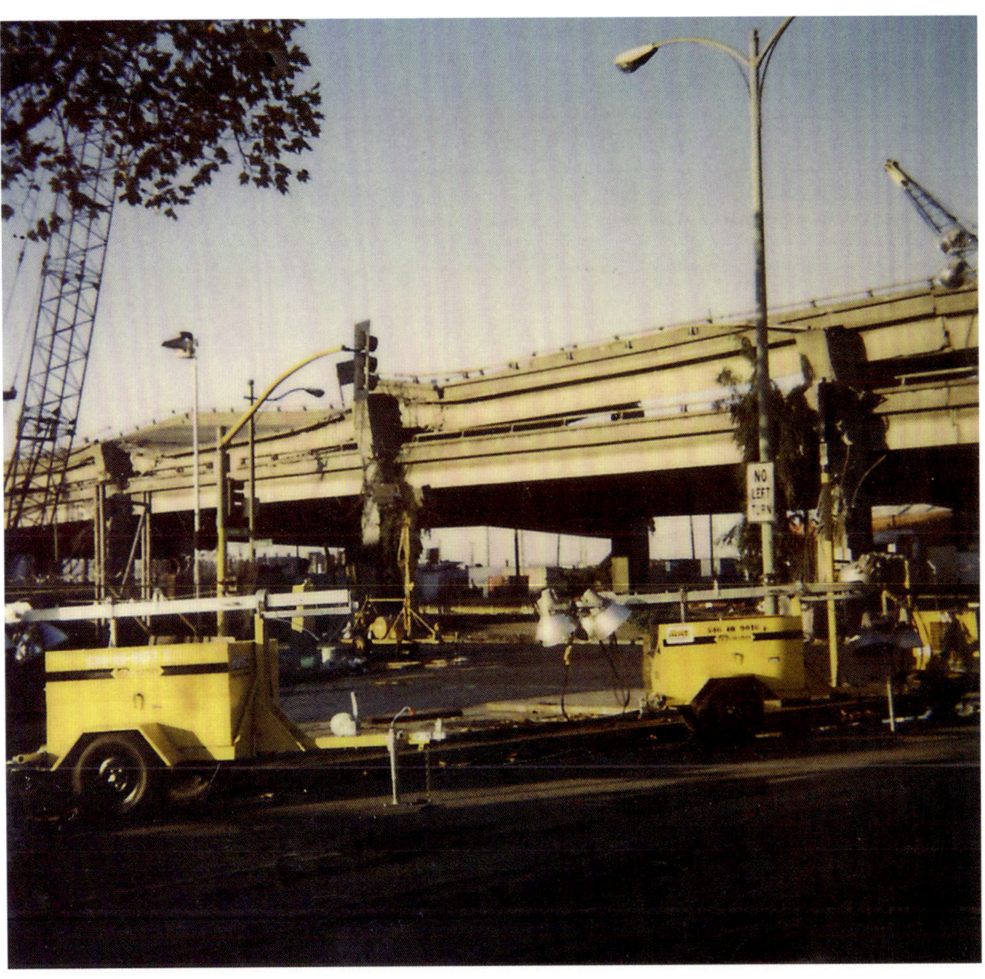

Small photographs do not do justice to the scale of the destruction. This photograph shows a section of the viaduct where the top deck has collapsed onto the lower deck, but not to the ground. The cars on the lower deck were not badly damaged but were stranded until iron workers could lift them out with cranes. The yellow generators and light poles in the foreground are so work can continue at night.

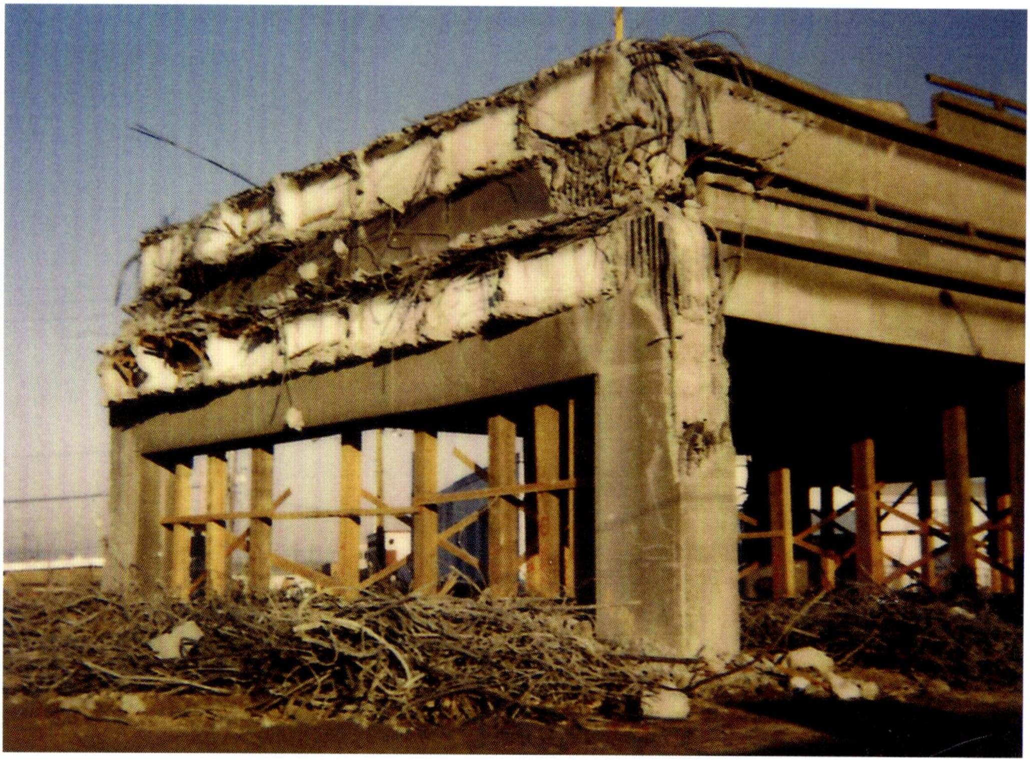

The damaged freeway was demolished section by section. Destroyed cars were removed and the rebar was separated from the concrete and sent to a steel recycling yard. (Photograph by John V. Robinson.)

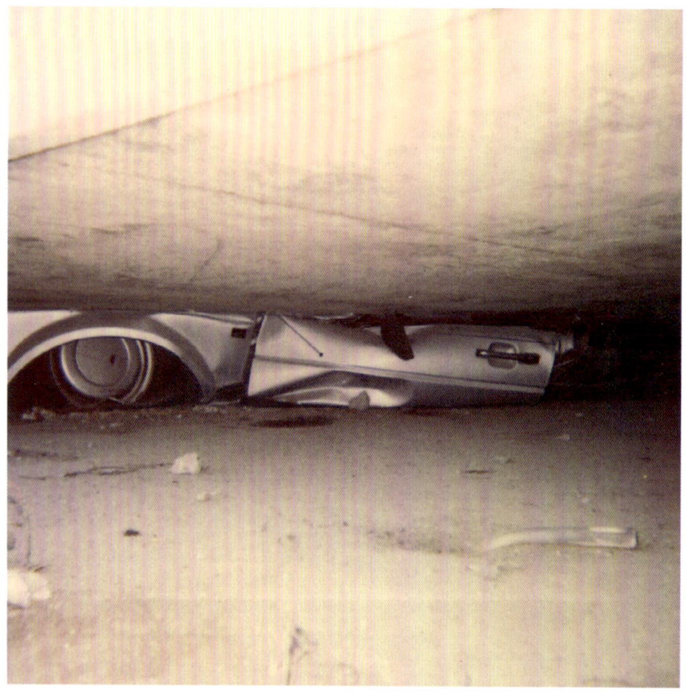

Other sections of the viaduct collapsed to the ground, crushing cars, and in some cases, their drivers. Cadaver dogs were used to find cars with deceased occupants. The driver of this car escaped unharmed, but the car is a total loss. (Photograph by John V. Robinson.)

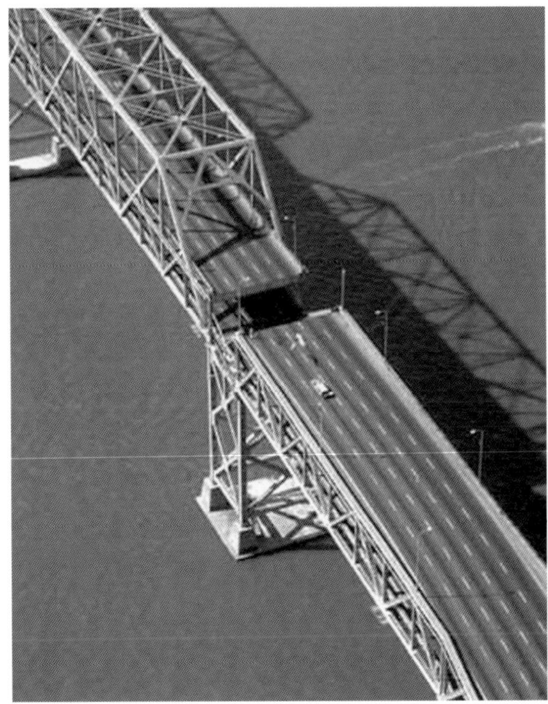

The most disruptive part of the 1989 earthquake was when this 50 -foot section of the westbound upper deck of the Bay Bridge collapsed onto the lower deck, which itself collapsed partially. The bridge is the main artery between the east bay and San Francisco. Public transport, such as buses, BART, and commuter ferries, were strained to capacity during the bridge repairs. To the credit of all involved, the bridge was repaired (with the addition of a protective troll) and open to traffic only thirty-one days after the earthquake. It seems now that the bridge designer designed the bridge to fail at this point to protect it against even greater damage from earthquakes. (Courtesy of the Library of Congress.)

The remains of the Cypress Freeway went away, never to return. Eventually the whole freeway interchange was rebuilt and rerouted, but that took years. Now that space is an open boulevard called Nelson Mandela Parkway.

The Bay Bridge was a different story. It was a major artery from the East Bay into San Francisco. It had to be repaired … fast. And it was! Local contractor Rigging International got the contract to repair the bridge. Bridge parts for a fifty-year old bridge cannot be purchased at the hardware store. The replacement parts had to be custom made, locally, and fast. That's where Stolz Metals, Michael Bondi, and Bill Roan come into the story.

2

BILL ROAN, MIKE BONDI, AND THE BAY BRIDGE GETS A TROLL

> Behold, I Myself have created the smith who blows the fire of coals and brings out a weapon for its work.
>
> (Isaiah 54:16)

Bill Roan, like many artists, is a rather mercurial type. When the troll was created, his attitude was to do something to commemorate the men and women who toiled to repair the damaged bridge so quickly. He wanted the troll to be an acknowledgment of their labor and to protect the bridge, the workers and the Bay Area commuters from the effects of any future earthquake. So he was happy when the little figure was placed in an inconspicuous location; "Where only the bridge painters and iron workers go. Nobody else would need to see it" is how Roan put it to me in a 2016 interview.

Bill Roan, 2016:

After World War Two we didn't need blacksmiths anymore and it was a dying art form. And that's kind of how I got involved. I grew up in Michigan, when I was in college, Eastern Michigan University. This was about 1978 and I was maybe

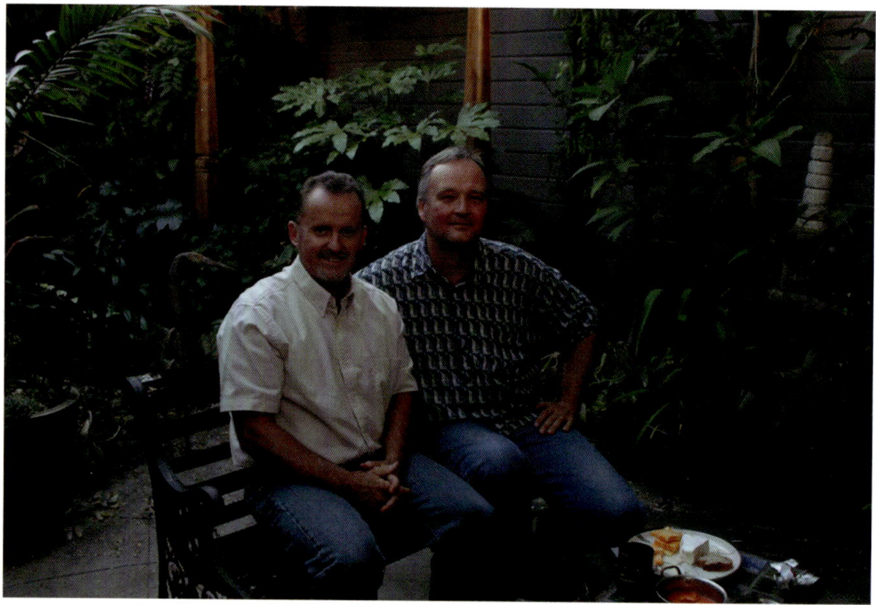

Author John Robinson and Bill Roan at Roan's Oakland home in April of 2016. Roan shared stories of his blacksmith training and shared photographs of some of his early work leading up to the Bay Bridge Troll. (Author's Collection.)

twenty-two. There was this colorful and gruff guy, named David Holtslander, who was getting his master's degree in metal work and I used to stand around watching him work at the forge. The roar of the fire, flying sparks, or as they are historically known as the Devil's fleas, would settle on bare forearms and flannel shirts, the repetitive sound of the hammer shaping the hot metal, and the sizzle of hot metal as it was cooled in the slack tub was the most dangerous and exciting thing I had ever seen. I'd stand and watch him for hours. I don't know if he saw something in me; that my interest was real, or if he thought I was being annoying, but one day he give me a piece of steel one inch square and eight inches long and said, "You don't get to stand around there staring at me, start hammering and make something. Over time David showed me how to build and tend a fire, split the metal, upset it, and draw it out. Most importantly, he showed me how to repair my mistakes, as I would repeatedly burn the end off the thin tapper in the fire. It took me about three weeks to make, but this was my first piece of work, a "homunculus."

Now the story of the homunculus is that a wizard would take his hair, sperm, and blood, and mix it all together and incubate it at 98 degrees for nine months. Then he'd take this waxy substance and form a figure, it would come alive, and become his alter-ego. This little creature would go into enemy camps and spy for the wizard. Well, a lot of my blood and hair went into making this figure as I was constantly burning and cutting myself. I am convinced if I added the third element it would come alive. But I'm not ready to try it.

During my college days, I got a minor in art history and I took a course on Asian Art and was deeply influenced by Japanese mythology, and the Netsuke Ivory carving that exemplify these beautiful works of folklore. A lot of my ideas are influenced by old myths and legends from around the world.

At the same time, I was exploring the ideas of the Patron Saints in the Catholic religion. Living in a Mexican enclave of Oakland, I noticed chickens running free in the alleys and I asked my Aunt Mary, who grew up in this neighborhood, "What's up with all these chickens running around?" She got upset and started yelling, "Chicken fighters, them damn Mexicans are all Chicken Fighters." This exchange got me thinking, Mexico is a Catholic country, they have patron saints for every occupation—who is the patron saint of chicken fighters, what would it look like?

With the string of small earthquakes we had that fall, I began to formulate the image of an Earthquake God. It seemed that it should be dancing and every time its foot struck the ground it would cause an earthquake. This image was probably influenced by my wife, Cynthia, who took up Flamenco dancing and her fast-paced stumping could really get our apartment shaking.

It had been extremely hot for days and there was talk around the shop of it being earthquake weather. When the earthquake struck the building, everyone was wrapping up for the day; I could hear a radio in the background, and there was talk of the start of the World Series. The earthquake struck like a freight train,

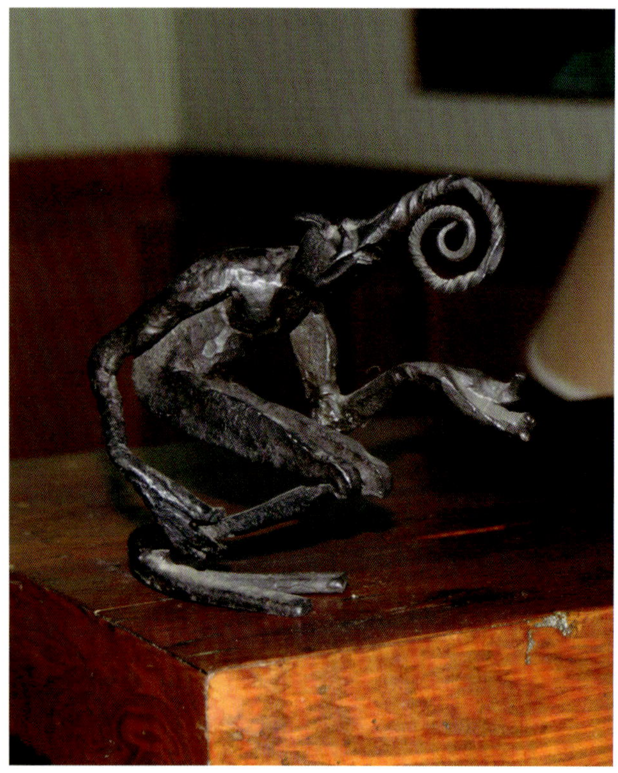

Roan's first creation at the forge was this little figure that he calls the "homunculus." (Photo by John V. Robinson.)

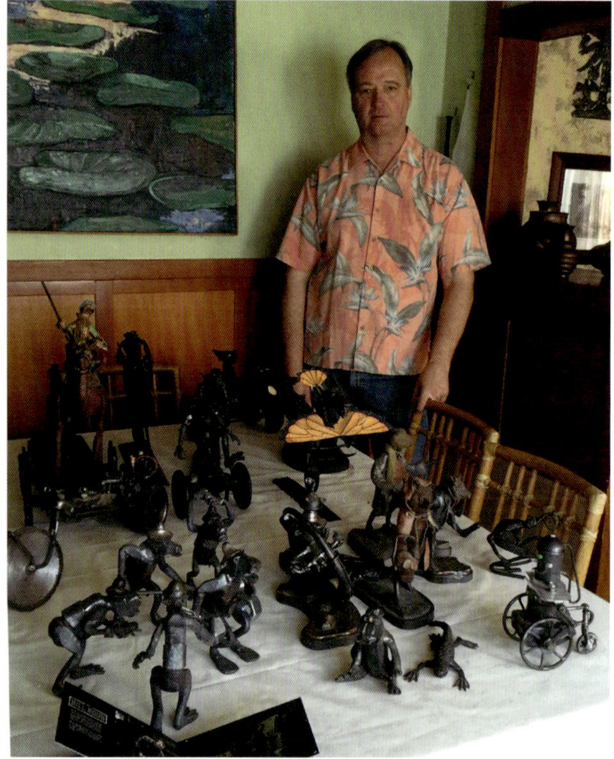

Bill Roan with some of his more recent whimsical creations that adorn his Oakland home. (Courtesy of Bill Roan.)

loud and like you were standing next to the tracks. Two Czechoslovakian tourists needed some money and Mike hired them under the table to do odd jobs for a couple of weeks. When the shaking hit, they ran up to me and shouted, "What is Daz?" At first I didn't know, and then I yelled, "Earthquake!" The first Czech got so excited that he ran right through me, it being the most direct way out of the building. I spun and caught myself; I pushed off the ground and attempted to get back on my feet, when the second Czech hit me, sending me face first to the ground. By the time I got back on my feet, I looked up to see both Czechs joining the Stoltz workers at the front door. I was on the 50-yard line and began to run for the front door. Time began to slow down and I felt like my own hero in an action movie. The metal rafters were shuttering back and forth, releasing 60 years of dust and grime, then the fluorescent tubes released from their fixtures, raining tubes of glass down around me as I ran in and out of the Stoltz Labyrinth of welders, saw-horses, trash cans, and gas tanks. When I finally got outside and joined the others, we were looking at each other and then we started to jump up and down shouting, "Do it again, do it again." The two Czech guys never returned to the shop—they headed for safer ground.

I drove home the ground route and the only damage I saw were a few toppled chimneys. If I had looked left instead of to the right when I drove under the 880 flyover, I would have seen the superstructure pancaked on the roadway below.

When I got home, I went up to the apartment roof and saw smoke billowing up from the San Francisco Marina, 880 across from our building had turned into a parking lot, and International Boulevard became the main artery for commuters trying to get home to the suburbs. The whores, who patrolled our block, were offering end-of-the-world, half-off blowjobs, but no one was interested. Everyone just wanted to get home.

My wife Cynthia was working at Macy's in the city, the electricity was cut off, the phone lines were down, and I had no idea where she was or if she was alive. The sky had turned an eerie glow as the sun set, sending parts of the Bay Area into total darkness. That night I was worried about Cynthia's safety and a small battery

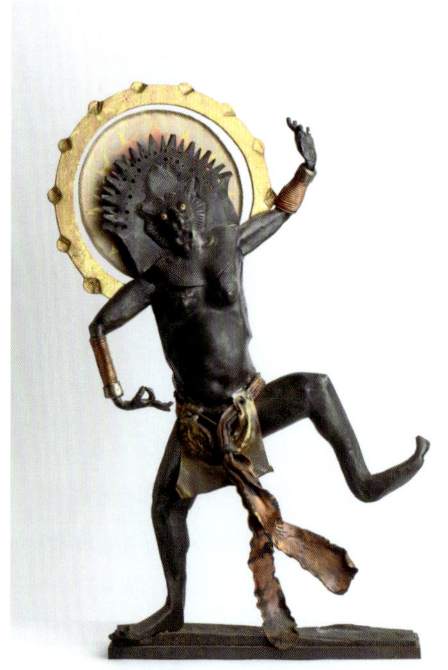

Roan's art is inspired by his general interest in mythology and folklore as well as his own fevered imagination. The best example of this is his San Andreas sculpture. Roan calls it "San Andreas the Earthquake God." Its dimensions are 24"x18"x6". This piece was started a week after the 1989 earthquake. Inspired by depictions of a Hindu God, every time San Andreas stumps his foot he causes an earthquake. Mike Bondi suggested this for the bridge repairs, but Roan came up with the troll idea instead. (Courtesy of Bill Roan.)

powered radio announced that the Bart was shut down for fear the tunnel under the bay may be flooding, the Marina District in San Francisco was on fire, and the Bay Bridge had collapsed. I wondered how so-called, primitive cultures cope with major catastrophes and I realized it's the artists who give their communities relief. By creating images that represent the forces that have caused them pain, people can point and say that's who did it to us, they are the ones responsible. That night I visualized "San Andreas the Earthquake God," and I couldn't wait to get back to work to start forging this new piece.

Cynthia, along with her fellow Macy's employees, fled the building after the earthquake and soon found they were locked out and weren't allowed to return to their lockers to get their purses. So they were trapped in the city with no money and nowhere to go. Luckily one of her coworkers rounded up as many women as he could fit in his car and took them to his apartment in the Castro for the night.

A few days after the earthquake, Stoltz Metals got the contract to make the replacement parts for the damaged section of the Bay Bridge. Caltrans reps, Rigging International engineers, inspectors, and other contractors were coming into the building every day to have meetings with Stoltz Metals. Mike Bondi was friends with Howard Stoltz and so Mike would sit in on some of their meetings. So, one day Bondi came from a meeting with Stoltz and the Caltrans inspector and said to me, "Hey, let's put that Earthquake figure you are making on the bridge. I think it would be fun."

As I recall, it took about a month to manufacture the replacement parts for the bridge. People were coming and going, and guys were working tremendous hours to get the work done as quickly as possible.

Now, I still had no intention of making anything for the bridge and the last week of the repair work. I had no idea what I was going to make, so after work and went to the library to research earthquake mythology and folklore. The only thing I could find was a Chinese tale that said something like, "Beneath the earth there dwells a dragon, who is bound with chains and ropes. Every time it tries to break its bindings, its struggle causes an earthquake." For an artist, what an image—imagine a fearsome Chinese dragon coiling, bound with ropes and chains— it would have been beautiful. But then I thought how that image might play badly back in the Midwest; San Francisco already had a bad reputation with kinky sexual behavior, what would the rest of the country say about a dragon in bondage?

So, I had no ideas at all. As I was driving home I remembered an old childhood favorite, "The Billy Goats Gruff." It was a story about a grumpy old troll who took very good care of his bridge. The next night I started forging and carving the head and body. I didn't know where it would be placed on the bridge, how big it would be, or what kind of pose it would take. The only thing I could do was make parts and hope I would get the proportions right.

The head was going to have goat horns in reference to the Billy Goats in the old story. I wanted to make this troll so fierce that it would scare away any earthquake that might come this way again. I thought of the New Zealand Maori, a fierce war-like people, who stick out their tongues and grimace toward any new stranger that might try to approach them. My troll would have a long tongue and grimace as well. Finally, I wanted a dragon head in honor of the Chinese dragon who lives beneath the earth.

That night as the Stoltz workers were walking back and forth, they would walk up to me and ask, "Is that what you are going to make for the bridge?" I would look up and say," Yes, it is." The word spread quickly, and I was surrounded by the workers as I continued carving the head. Craig, the foreman, had to break up the circle because all work on the bridge stopped for the moment.

The next day, word of the troll got back to Bondi, and he wanted to get in on the act, so Wednesday night he decided to make his own figure. He talked about doing an egg-head figure with a slide rule and do a caricature of California Governor Deukmejian, because he felt it was the fault of the original engineers and the Governor for the bridge failing during the earthquake. I just wanted to honor all the hardworking people that were involved with the reconstruction.

The next morning, Mike came up to me and said, "Hey Bill, I want you to let the other guys help out with the troll." And I said, "I 've got it pretty much done, there's not much to do." But Mike insisted, saying, "It would mean so much to them." The foreman, Art Jones, had been head blacksmith at the Mare Island Navy Yard. He was in charge of forging submarine parts. And the other smith was Frank Trousil from Czechoslovakia. So I asked Art to make a spud wrench, and I heated up the head and held a punch in its mouth while Frank gave it two or three whacks to extend the groove down the middle of the tongue. After work, Stoltz's foreman Craig showed me where it could be placed on the bridge. The Caltrans inspector had said it would need to be placed on the outside of the bridge so that it wouldn't cause traffic jams, because people would be looking for it once it became known to the public.

I took the parts and tack welded them together in place, and then took it back to the Bondi shop to finish welding, grinding, and painting. I stamped BAY BRIDGE

TROLL 1989 on Art's spud wrench. It's not a real spud wrench. (He fabricated it out of a piece of steel, forged it to a tapper, then punched out a hole and put in the dog-leg, so it would look right.) I'd never seen a spud wrench before I saw the Stolz guys using them to align the bridge steel. They stick the pointed end into the bolt holes to pry the sections into alignment.

Friday morning, I showed Art and Frank the finished piece and Art told me I needed to sign my name and I said it wasn't necessary; it would be so high up that no one would be able to read it. But Art insisted so I got the stamps out and signed "Artist William Roan."

Mike had showed up and was hovering around looking over my shoulder. I handed him the hammer and told him he should put the shop name on the other washer. After he was done, he picked up two more stamps and struck them one on top of the other next to his name. It was a copyright symbol and he said, "We don't want anyone to steal our idea."

I handed the finished troll over to Craig and he loosely bolted the troll on to the last bridge section. They didn't want to put it on permanently, just in case Caltrans might order it off. So that morning, the last retrofitted section, with the attached troll, was loaded on to a flatbed to be delivered to the bridge. I remember me and Mike Bondi climbing up onto the trailer and posing next to the troll before it left the shop. Then all the Stroltz workers gathered on to the flatbed for their pictures. The guys wanted me to join them, because I was one of them—I had made the troll for them.

A few hours later, Howard Stoltz returned from the bridge and told me the morning events. The truck pulled up to the delivery point and all the bridge workers gathered round to admire the troll that was fastened to the bridge. Paula Drake from KGO talk radio was on the bridge trying to figure out an angle to finish the story of the bridge: earthquake hits bridge, bridge falls down, bridge is rebuilt, end of story. But now the bridge has protective troll to scare away future earthquakes. Paula got so excited that she started calling everyone in the news business she knew and by the time the news got to the east coast, the news

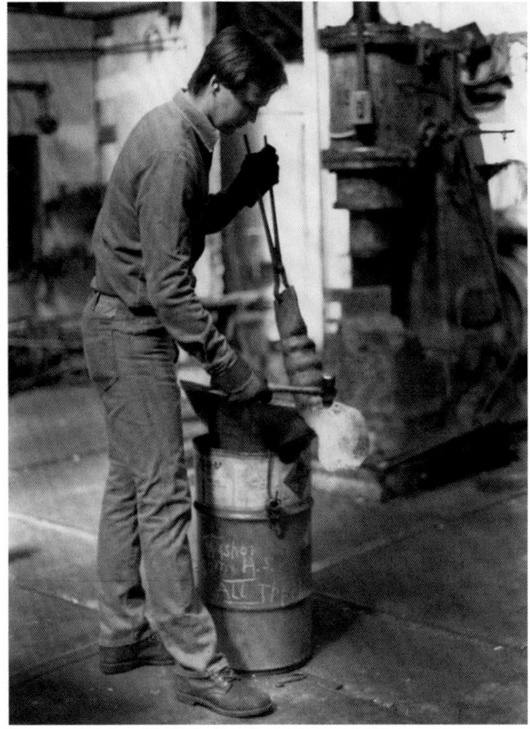

Bill Roan, *circa* 1989, with hammer and tongs, at work on one of his many creations. (Courtesy of Bill Roan.)

affiliates were calling back to find out who the bridge rigger was that put this 40-foot sculpture on the side of the bridge. As the story was told and retold, my 18-inch sculpture had grown in size.

When the reporters got out to the bridge, doing interviews and taking pictures, one of them called Caltrans in Sacramento to see what they thought of a troll being attached to the Bay Bridge. Of course, the official didn't know anything about it and said, "I don't know anything about a troll and if there is a troll on the bridge we'll take it off." Well the reporter went back to the group of people admiring the troll and told them what the Caltrans official said. The workers said, "No they're not." And then they welded the piece onto the bridge. Then they heated up the bolt's threats and peened them over. Howard laughed and said, "There, if they want to take it off they will have to crawl over the side and cut it off themselves, because we [the iron workers] are not going to do it."

That evening, the local press and TV news showed up at the shop to interview the artist who made the troll. Mike pulled me aside and said, "I will introduce you as the artist, but I will do all the talking." Mike stepped forward to greet the press and they didn't want anything to do with him. They wanted to talk to me. So after that, when a reporter called, Mike would take the call—he controlled the phones in his shop and he determined how the story would be spun.

Stoltz's guys wanted me to make them a troll, and when Rigging International asked that I make them another Bay Bridge Troll, something had to be done. I didn't make the troll to turn a profit; I made it to honor everyone that worked so hard to get the Bay Area back on its feet after the earthquake. So, when Bondi told me Stoltz wanted me to make another troll for Rigging International. I asked a ridiculously low price of $250. A few months later, I walked into Mike's office to verify a detail on a project I was working on and I heard Mike say on the phone, "Yeah, I made the second troll too." He turned and started waving his arm for me to get out of his office.

A few weeks later, I joined Frank and Art in the shop and neither one of them would make eye contact with me. I asked them what was wrong and showed me a magazine article where Mike had been interviewed and he claimed to have made both trolls. Mike's defense was, "Anything that comes out of my shop belongs to me." So, you can imagine our working relationship didn't last much longer.

At the time I made the troll I never thought we'd be talking about twenty-five years later. I had no idea what would be come of it. I thought Caltrans would remove it immediately. Or it would be stolen. I didn't think it would stay on the bridge for two decades.

Mike Bondi on the 1989 troll:

In 1989, I had an artist blacksmith shop in Oakland in the old Phoenix Iron Works building. I shared a large shop space with Stoltz Metals, a large steel fabrication company. There was a 30,000-square-foot space. I had 5,000 square feet. And Stoltz had most of the rest of it.

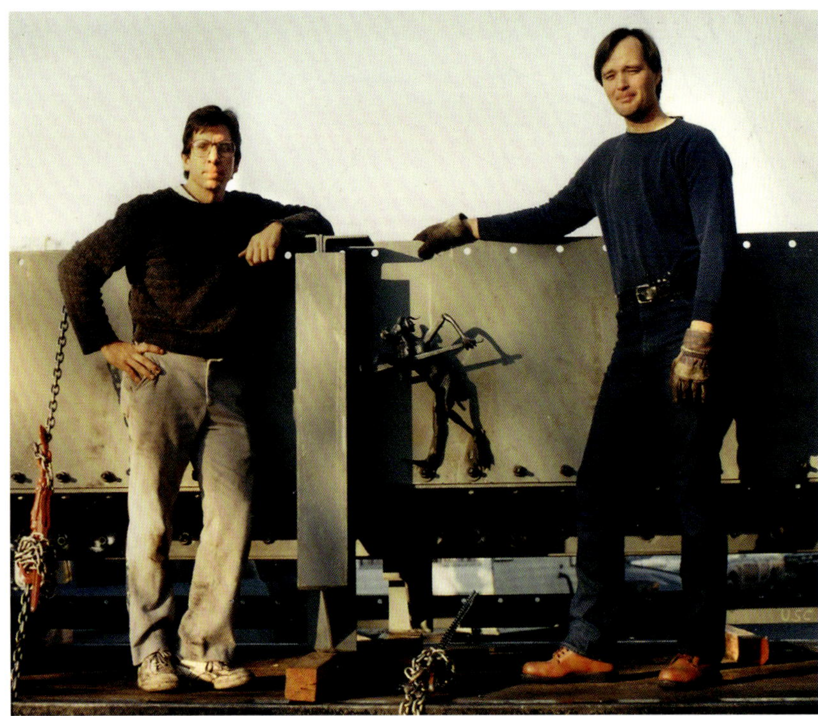

Mike Bondi (left) and Bill Roan (right) with the Bay Bridge Troll in November 1989. The troll is mounted on one of the final pieces to go onto the bridge. The state was eager to open the bridge as soon as possible. Placing the troll at the last minute made the prospects of removal less likely. Caltrans would have no time to react. If everything would have gone according to plan, the troll would have gone onto the bridge with no fanfare and the bridge workers would have been the only ones to see or know of its existence. As it turns out, Paula Drake, a reporter for KCBS News Radio, was there that day and broadcast the troll's existence to the world. (Courtesy of Mike Bondi.)

The building was very close to the Cypress Freeway and the bridge, so when the bridge collapsed, Stoltz Metals was contacted by GO Supply and Rigging International about building and staging some of the repair parts. Howard Stoltz and I got to inspect the broken section just a few days after the collapse.

I happened to be sitting in Howard's office during a meeting with Caltrans, George Osher, and others, when I suggested that what the bridge needed was a protector, like a gargoyle on a cathedral that I could make out of forged steel.

We talked about it for a while, and they all said it sounded like a great Idea. I had in mind a gargoyle-type creature similar to ones I had seen in Europe on the cathedrals. Now I was originally thinking of a political caricature of someone, like then Governor Deukmejian, because the medieval stone carvers would put the face of the pope or something like that on their work.

I went out to my shop and told my crew (who all did blacksmithing), Art Jones, Frank Trousil, Bill Roan, and Felipe Vasquez, that we had a chance to do something fun and anyone who had a good idea should speak up. Now the guys who worked in my shop were free to use my shop and equipment to work on their own projects after hours.

Bill Roan was really into doing figurative stuff like that. That was his thing. It's not really my thing to do figurative stuff. Now at that time Bill Roan had already done a bunch of figurative sculptures which were really nice. He was working on a piece called San Andreas. My first instinct was to suggest we use one of those pieces that he had already completed. But Bill said no. Maybe he thought it was too big. He really thought Caltrans would never go for it. He also didn't care for the political caricature idea.

So, it kicked around for a few days, and then Bill Roan came into my office and asked if I remembered the story of the Three Billy Goats Gruff and the troll that lived under the bridge. We talked about it, and I told him it was a great idea and he should design it.

He came up with a design, and I insisted that everyone in the shop had to make a part or work on it. In the end, I had discussions with Stoltz, Caltrans reps, and George about how we should locate it so no one would see it and cause traffic problems. I also designed it to fit a bolt pattern, so no one could say we compromised any welds or the structure in any way. No one who had not been to Stoltz Metals knew of it or saw it till the morning it went up. I remember posing for a photograph with Bill, me, and the troll on the truck the day it was taken out to the bridge. The troll was on the outside of the northern most beam. It was where no commuters could see it and therefore could not cause traffic problems.

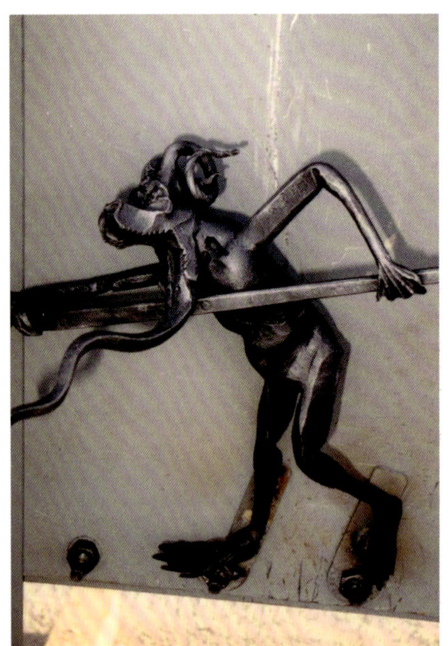

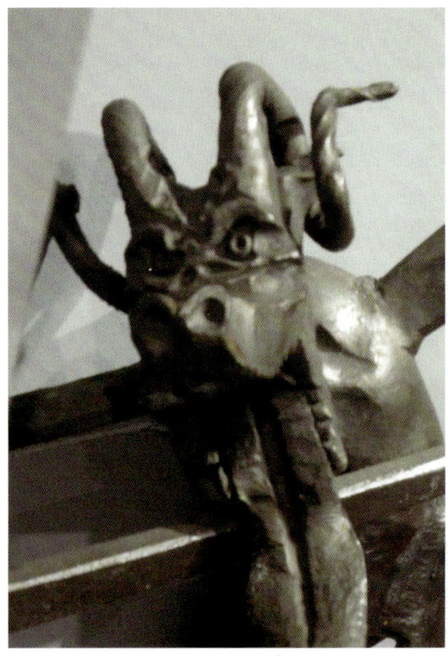

Above left: A Caltrans photographer was on duty to see the beam put into place. He snapped this photograph which became the official portrait of the Bay Bridge Troll. (Courtesy of Caltrans.)

Above right: A closeup view of the troll's face. (Author's collection.)

Once on the bridge, the iron workers loved it and they welded it to the bolts so it could not be easily removed

There were reporters on the scene who asked about the troll and photographed it. There was one particular reporter, Paula Drake from KCBS News Radio, who saw it and broadcasted it on the radio. I think that may have been first publicity the troll got. The next thing I knew it was all over the news. After the word got out, Caltrans had to comment and there was some talk about removing it, but as we all know, it stayed. And that was that. It got its fifteen minutes of fame. Now, I stamped my copyright on it so no one else could take the image and use it. I never intended to claim ownership I just wanted to protect it from others who might try to use it for personal gain. It's a piece of public art. I think Bill Roan feels the same way.

Also, I was not paid any money for the troll. It was a gift from my business and me to the city. I was asked by George Osher to make a second troll for Rigging

International to put in their office. So I put him in touch with Bill Roan and I believe Bill made that troll on his own time in the shop. I had George pay him directly as a reward for a great design of that first troll. I got nothing from the first troll. My shop wasn't even involved in the bridge repairs. It was just circumstance that I got involved at all. It was a labor of love a gift to the people who worked day and night repairing the old bridge.

Its future is foggy, but I would like to be sure its history is clear. That's why I agreed to talk to you. The concept and idea to put a guardian on the bridge was mine, the design was Bill Roan's, and it was a good one. It was made by everyone working for me at the time a collaborative effort, just like the bridge repair.

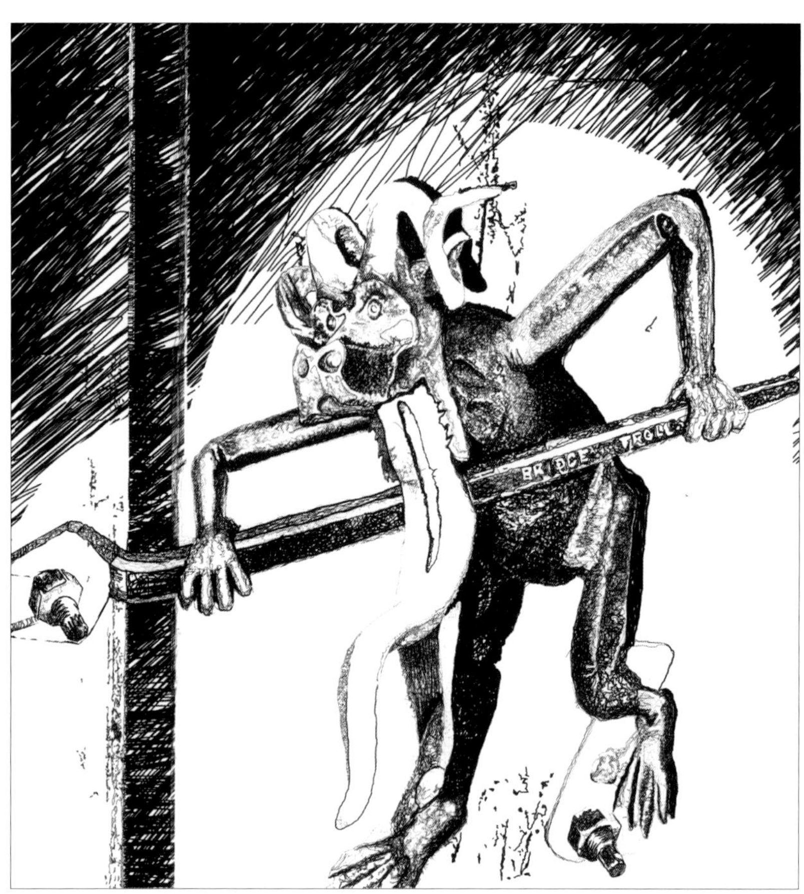

(Troll drawing by Bill Roan.)

3

"FISH"

My name is James Sturgeon and people call me "Fish" for obvious reasons. I was working for American Bridge on the new Bay Bridge, and as the bridge was almost ready to open there were rumors and questions floating around the job, and people were wondering what was going to happen to the old troll. I remember hearing about the old troll as a kid. I don't recall how or where. I just knew about it. When we were working on the new bridge we'd have occasion to see it. It was directly across from the south deck of the eastbound lanes of the new bridge, as big as life.

Now, American Bridge/Flour were contracted to build the new bridge, not to demo the old bridge. But knowing the history of the troll, and what is symbolizes, in protecting the old bridge. As a bridge worker, we take a lot of pride in our work. We, the iron workers, felt we had the right, the duty, to remove that troll.

One afternoon the general superintendent, Jerry Kent, came to me and asked, "Would you like to be part of removing that old troll?" And I thought that was a good honor. So, we talked about how we might do it and what we might need. I knew the diameter to the handrail pipe above the troll, so I made a kind of fireman's ladder with hooks at the top to swallow the handrail.

That weekend they closed the bridge to traffic, so they could do the lane switch to transition traffic to the new bridge. The idea was to take five days to reconfigure the traffic on the Oakland side and then have the new bridge open for commuters after the long Labor Day weekend. That first night we got in our gear truck and posted up near the bridge. Now these contactor trucks all kind of look the same big white truck, full of tools, with flashing yellow lights on top. We thought no one would really notice. We were waiting for the all clear call to come over the radio telling us that the old bridge was shut down and the crews could go to work making the lane switch to direct traffic onto the new bridge. They had five days to get the bridge open again. We were hoping everybody would be too busy to notice what we were up to.

As soon as we heard the all clear, we took off, me and a mechanic in his truck, with an engineer and the general superintendent following in another truck. No one was suspicious. We knew right where the troll was. It was the last deck panel right before the camel back segments started on the old bridge. We pulled up next to where the troll was, I looked over the side of the bridge and there it was. I got my tool belt and harness, put the ladder over the side with the grappling hooks attached to the top rail, and climbed over the side. I knew we wouldn't have much time before someone noticed us and started asking questions. That happened quicker than we thought. I guess other people had the same idea as us.

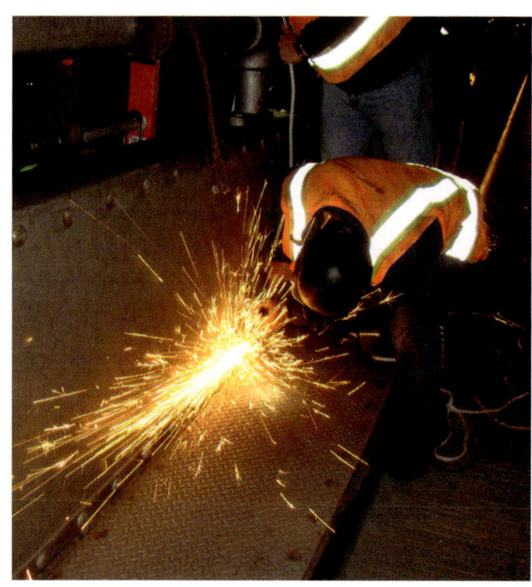

An iron worker uses a grinding wheel to quickly shear of the bolt-heads holding the troll in position on the far side of the beam. (Courtesy of James Sturgeon.)

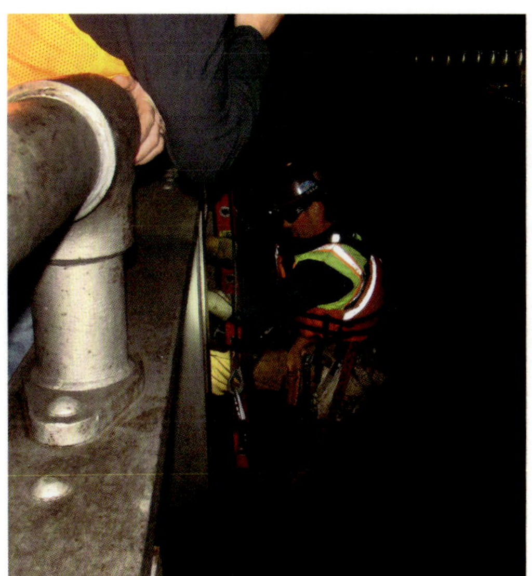

On the far side of the beam, iron worker James "Fish" Sturgeon waits to break through the years of paint and corrosion to free the little troll from the bridge. The new bridge is in the background. (Courtesy of James Sturgeon.)

The troll was attached to the steel in three places: two small mounting plates at the troll's feet that were aligned to the bolt holes of the beam, and, at top, the little spud wrench the toll is holding was attached to a bolt along the side of the beam. Now these are Lejeune bolts that have a rounded head so they look like rivets from the back side. Anyway, the troll had been welded to the nut side of the bolts, so I figured the quickest way to get him off was to cut the bolt heads with a cut-off wheel on a grinder.

After we got the bolt-heads off, we put the ladder back over the edge and I climbed over to tie a safety rope around the troll. Then the guys up top began using pins and a sledgehammer to drive the bolts out and free the troll.

I tied off the troll so it wouldn't fall. I got the first two bolts out and I heard some trucks rolling up and heard some yelling. Then a CHP officer poked his head over the side and said, "Stop what you're doing! What are you trying to steal?"

"I'm not stealing anything." I told him. "I'm just here to get the troll." The cop did not know what the heck I was talking about. He was younger than me, which made me feel old, and he'd never heard of the Bay Bridge Troll.

Meanwhile other contractor trucks and CHPs were arriving on the scene and people were arguing about who had the rights to the troll. It looked like everyone had the same idea. Get that troll! But we got there first. We'd brought a mechanics truck, we had a generator, torches, every kind of tool, so we were prepared for anything when I climbed over the side. That troll had been there for something like twenty-four years and we didn't know what shape it would be in painted over a dozen times or rusted in place? We just didn't know.

So various people (contractors) were claiming rights to the troll. Eventually a cop poked his head over the side of the bridge and told me to climb back up and to turn off the generator. "The troll is almost cut loose. It's tied off but there's not much holding it on anymore." I said, "What do you want me to do here?" If we left, it wouldn't take someone else but five minutes to break it loose and run off with it. So, they all started arguing again and with that distraction I had the generator switched back on and went over the side again and finished breaking loose the troll. Again, someone switched off the generator and again I was instructed to stop. But it was too late. I had the troll in my hands.

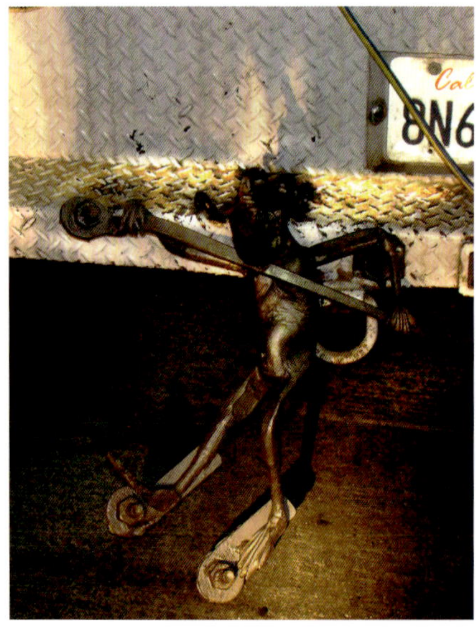

The man of the hour. The little troll poses for a photograph. As it turns out, sneaking the troll off the bridge was harder than sneaking it onto the bridge. (Courtesy of James Sturgeon.)

So, again, I asked them, "What do you want to do? I have the troll in my hands. I can drop it in the bay if you want." And people were yelling "No, no, don't drop it." That shook them up a bit.

After things calmed down a bit I climbed up the ladder with the troll and I handed it to Jerry Kent who untied the rope from it. By that time everyone had stopped yelling and screaming, and the mood had changed. Now everyone was "oohing" and "awing." By this time there were several people there: three or four CHPs, mechanics Gene Pratt and Joe Hernandez, Jerry Kent, Adam Reeve, Mark MacDonald, and me, with more showing up all the time. We were not the only ones to want that troll. We just got there first and brought gear trucks and mechanics with us. We would not be denied.

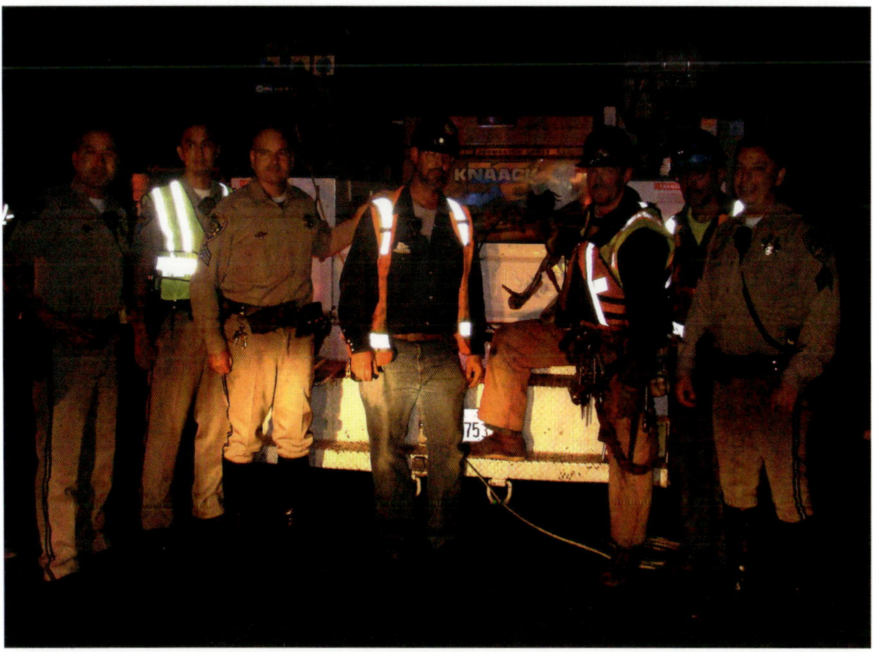

After some tense moments involving the California Highway Patrol, regarding who has the right to retrieve the troll, a custody agreement was reached and the assembled CHP officers, troll pirates, and other assorted claimants settled down to pose for photos with the troll and savor the moment. (Courtesy of James Sturgeon.)

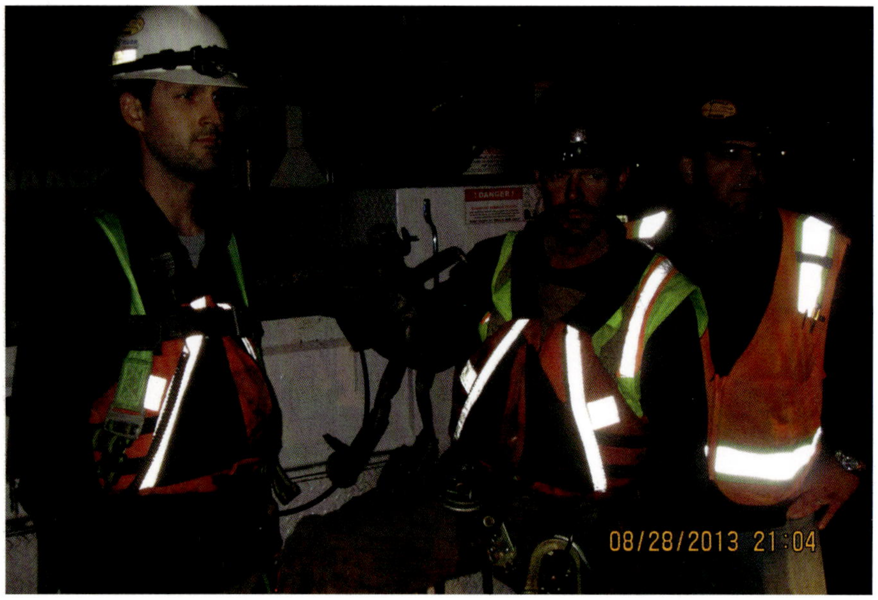

Adam Reeve (left), Fish Sturgeon (center), and Mark McDonald (right) pose with their prize. (Courtesy of James Sturgeon.)

So, we got the troll. But we did not make our getaway. Our plan was to remove the troll and mount it on a plate and present it to the Iron Worker's Local 378 the same guys that helped fix the old bridge after the 1989 quake. Now that things had calmed down a bit it was decided to take the troll back to the contractor's main office for safekeeping. It stayed there for a few days. About three days after we cut it loose, Jerry Kent called me into the office and the troll was there. Jerry said we got visitation rights, so I went in and posed with it one more time. Eventually Caltrans took possession of it and it was mounted on a beam, you know, like when it was on the bridge, and brought out to a couple of public events. At one of those events I met Bill Roan. That was pretty cool. I don't know where the troll is now.

Now, about the new troll I saw the new troll before we took down the old troll. One-day Brett and me were at work. This was before the new bridge was open. But it was pretty well finished. We were doing a punch list. That's a list

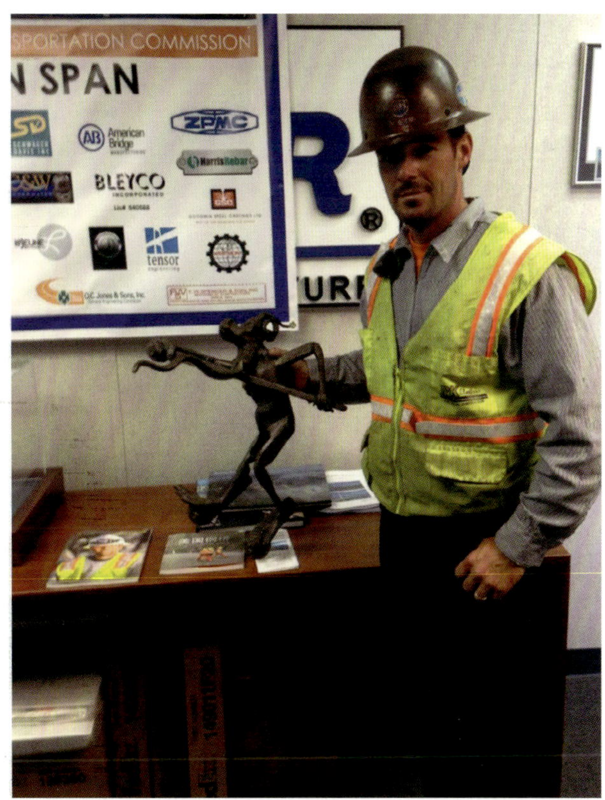

Right: A few days later, Sturgeon strikes a pose with the spruced-up troll. It was decided to show the troll at the bridge opening ceremony, so the troll was cleaned of twenty-four years of accumulated grime. (Courtesy of James Sturgeon.)

Below: At the opening ceremony for the new bridge, the old troll was a featured guest. People were invited to pose with the little troll. Here, Bill Roan (left), the troll's creator, meets James Sturgeon (right), the troll's liberator. (Courtesy of James Sturgeon.)

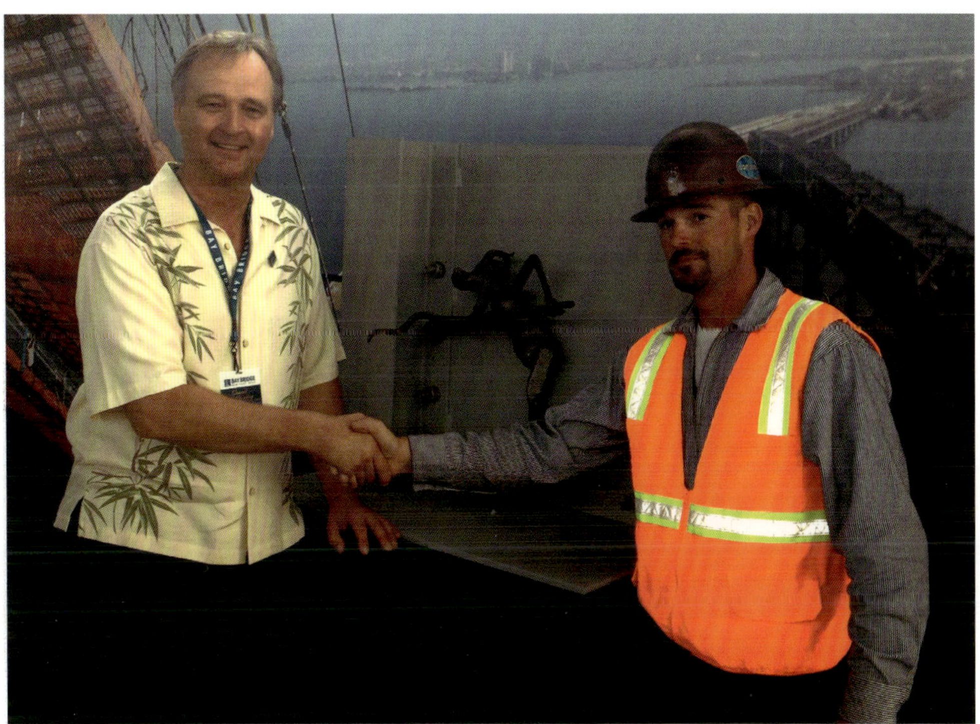

of a hundred little jobs that need to be done before the bridge is turned over to the State and they take over maintenance. I was working there two years after the bridge opened just completing the punch list. One day we were in one of the deck panels at one of the cross beams and we saw the new troll up there. It was wrapped in rope, like someone had pulled it up there and stashed it behind the cross beam so no one could see it. I didn't know what it was. I'd heard rumors that the old troll would be removed and installed on the new bridge. But there were many rumors floating around at that time. See, I'd also heard rumors there was a plan to make a fake troll. Steal the old troll and give Caltrans the fake one. So, what was this we were looking at? When I got back to the office I told a couple of people what I'd found and was told to keep quiet about it. Well, it turns out we had discovered the new troll. How it got there? I do not know.

In an unpublished typescript sent to Bill Roan, bridge engineer, Matthew Bruce, who was among the scrum contending for the old troll that night, claims they intended to take the old troll and mount it on the new bridge. I don't have permission to quote from Bruce's letter, so I will paraphrase briefly that Bruce

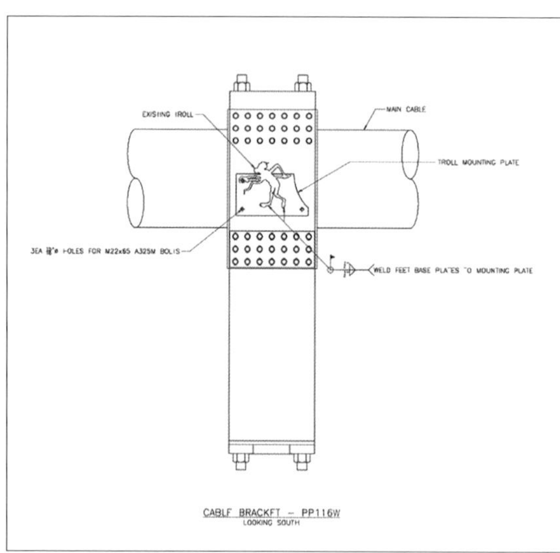

This technical drawing from the New Bay Bridge contractor, American Bridge/Flour, hints at what might have been. It is a preliminary technical drawing of how the old troll might have been placed on the new bridge. Until recently, I had assumed the new troll was placed on the bridge formally. But that seems not to be the case. This drawing was an informal plan to place the old troll on the new span. When the old troll was intercepted and fell into Caltrans' hands, this plan was scrapped, and the new troll came into play.

showed plan sheets [i.e. blueprints] that had been made for the placement of the old troll on the new bridge.

After phone calls, screaming, and a near fist fight, an agreement was reached that the iron workers would remove the troll and turn it over to Greg Allen, who would give it to management. Now some parts of this story don't square with Sturgeon's account of removing the troll to give to the iron workers. But it's quite possible they had different ideas of what would happen to the troll once they had it. And Sturgeon, who was over the side of the bridge much of the time, was in no position to hear the details of the negotiations.] At any rate, the troll ended up with Caltrans who mounted in on a beam and put it on display at the Oakland Museum, among other places.

4

A NEW BRIDGE, A NEW TROLL

> *The troll, in essence, is a protector, a good spirit. He was made as a token of respect for those people who worked hard at putting up the bridge.*
>
> *Mike Bondi*

In May 2014, a new troll was installed on the new bridge. Michael Bondi Metal Designs was invited to make the new troll for the new eastern span. In July 2017, I drove to Bondi's Richmond shop to ask him about the old troll, the new troll, and his thoughts about the media attention the little trolls have attracted.

Mike Bondi:

When the new bridge was nearing completion, I got a call from some of the guys, involved in making the old troll, telling me they wanted a new troll for the new bridge. That itself was controversial. I don't think it went through official channels. I think some folks in Caltrans wanted the old troll to go into a museum, and some wanted it to go on the new bridge. The public at large definitely wanted the old troll to go to the new bridge. I saw news articles about the old troll people spoke for saving the troll at public meetings.

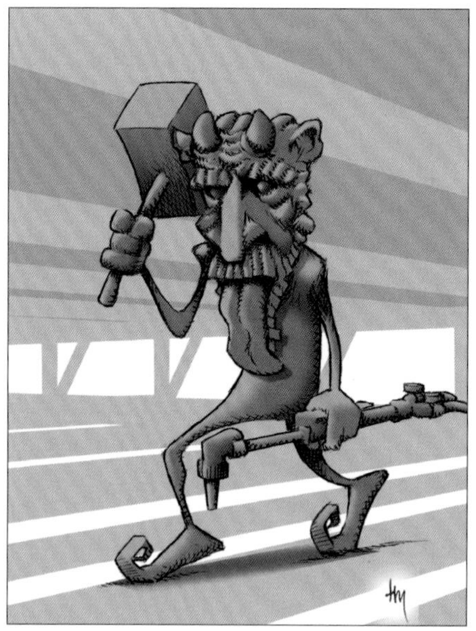

In July 2017, I contacted political cartoonist Tom Meyer to question him on the original Bay Bridge Troll's appearance in the *San Francisco Chronicle*. I asked him if he had ever used the new troll in a cartoon. He said no, but graciously offered to draw the new troll for me, which I am happy to publish here. (Courtesy of Tom Meyers.)

But for the new troll, there were no call for artists to submit designs. At least not that I ever heard of. It was basically the same group of guys that were involved with the first troll. They just said, "We're doing it!" So, they called me because I supplied the first troll. But there again, the artist hand ruled the day. Bill Roan never understood what I was after with that first troll. I wanted it to be a political statement. (I never demanded it be so, I just floated the idea. I thought that would be really cool.) But Bill created his troll, so that's what went on the bridge.

And as for the new troll, I was out of the country in Italy doing a demonstration when that new troll was made. Freddy Rodriguez, from Columbia, was up in California working in my shop. So I turned the project over to him and the rest of my guys. I gave them some instructions, made some suggestions, gave them a rough time frame, and told them to figure it out. I was somewhat annoyed that my guys didn't do what I suggested. But I wasn't here when they made the new creature, so I just thought "The hell with it. It's the artist hand. They get to do what they want." Still, it's a nice little figure. Beautiful work.

To be honest, I don't even know how the new troll got to the bridge: did someone from here deliver it, or did someone from the bridge pick it up from us? We had no formal connection to the new bridge. We didn't have a contract to make anything. Again, like in 1989, the sole contribution of Bondi Metals to the bridge was an ornamental troll.

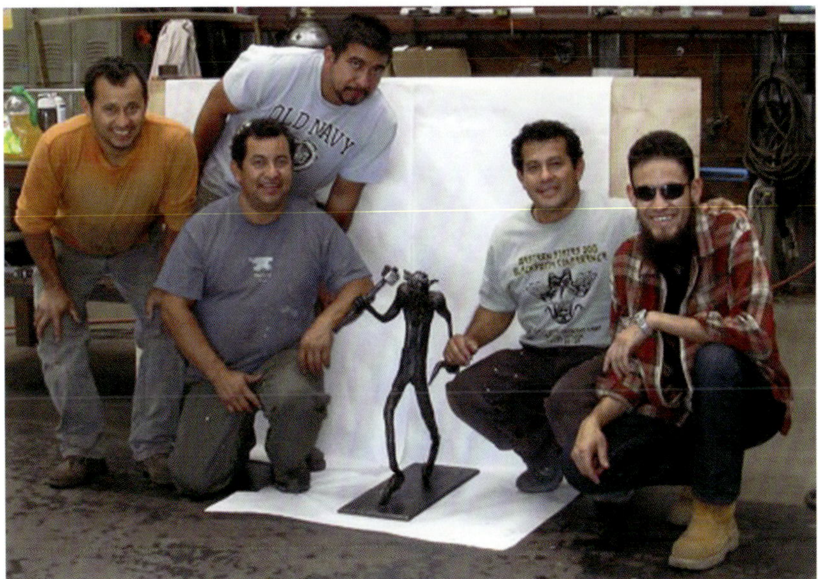

Michael Bondi Metal Design in Richmond, CA, made the new troll, called "Junior" in some circles. Here the team that made the new troll pose with their creation: Felipe Vasquez, Alfonso Vasquez, Socrates Vasquez, Humberto Somayoa, and Columbian blacksmith Freddy Rodriguez. Bondi says at his shop, they never called the new troll "Junior." Perhaps like the old troll, the new troll is taking on a life of its own in pop culture. (Courtesy of Michael Bondi Metal Design.)

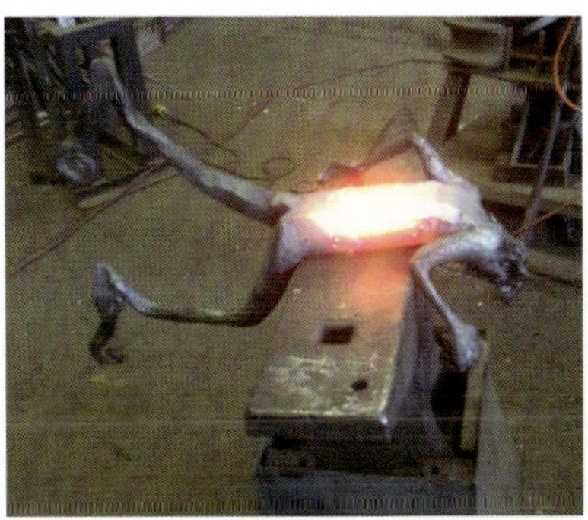

Here we see the new troll in Michael Bondi's Richmond shop. Laying across an anvil, the troll's back has been heated red hot, so the participants can punch their names into its back. (Courtesy Michael Bondi Metal Design.)

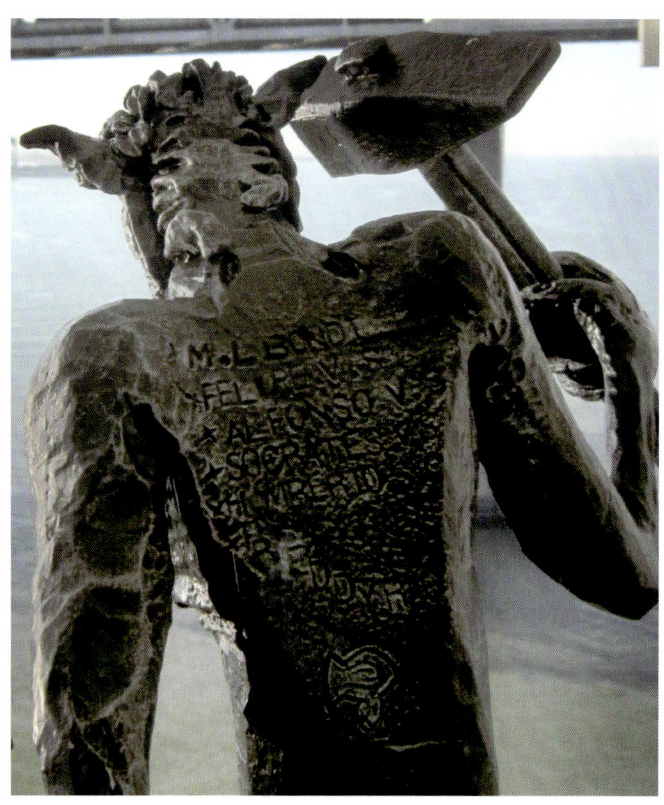

Left: Punched into the back of the new troll are the names of the team members who created it for Michael Bondi Metals. From top to bottom are:

x M.L. Bondi
x Felipe. V.S [Vasquez]
x Alfonso. V.S [Vasquez]
x Socrates. V.S [Vasquez]
x Humberto S. [Somayoa]
x Freddy R.O [Rodriguez
(Courtesy of James Sturgeon.)

Below: On Friday, May 9, 2014, the new troll was unveiled to a select audience of bridge workers who were tasked with its installation. Wielding a sledge hammer and clutching an oxyacetylene torch head, he appears to be ready for work deconstructing the old bridge in the background. (Courtesy of James Sturgeon.)

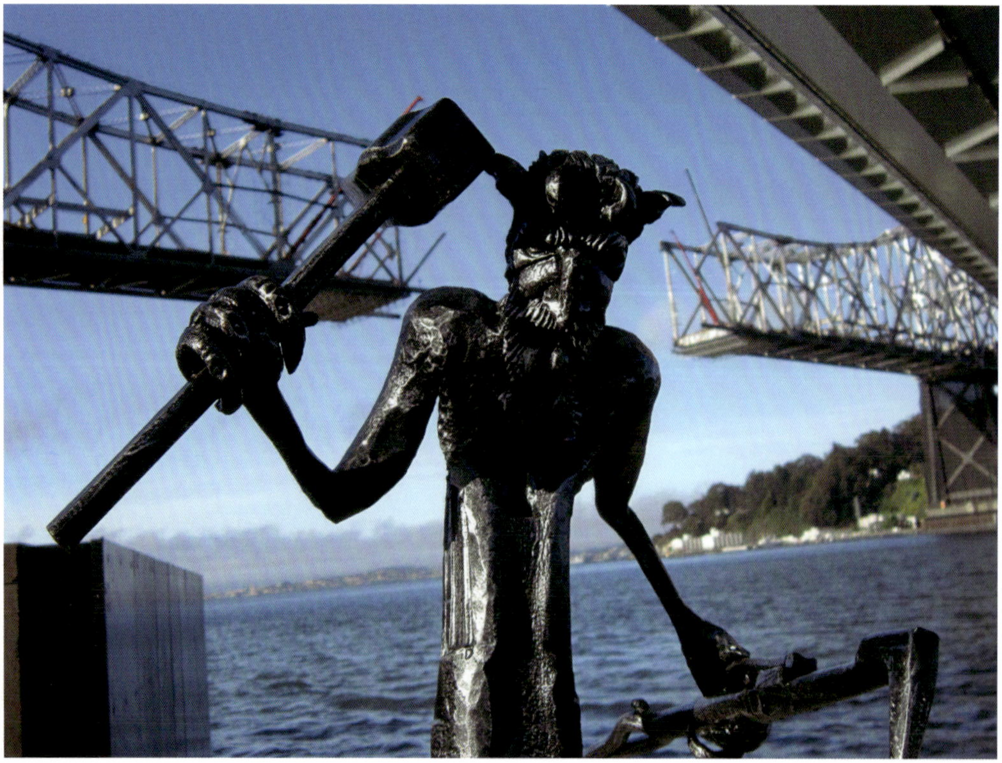

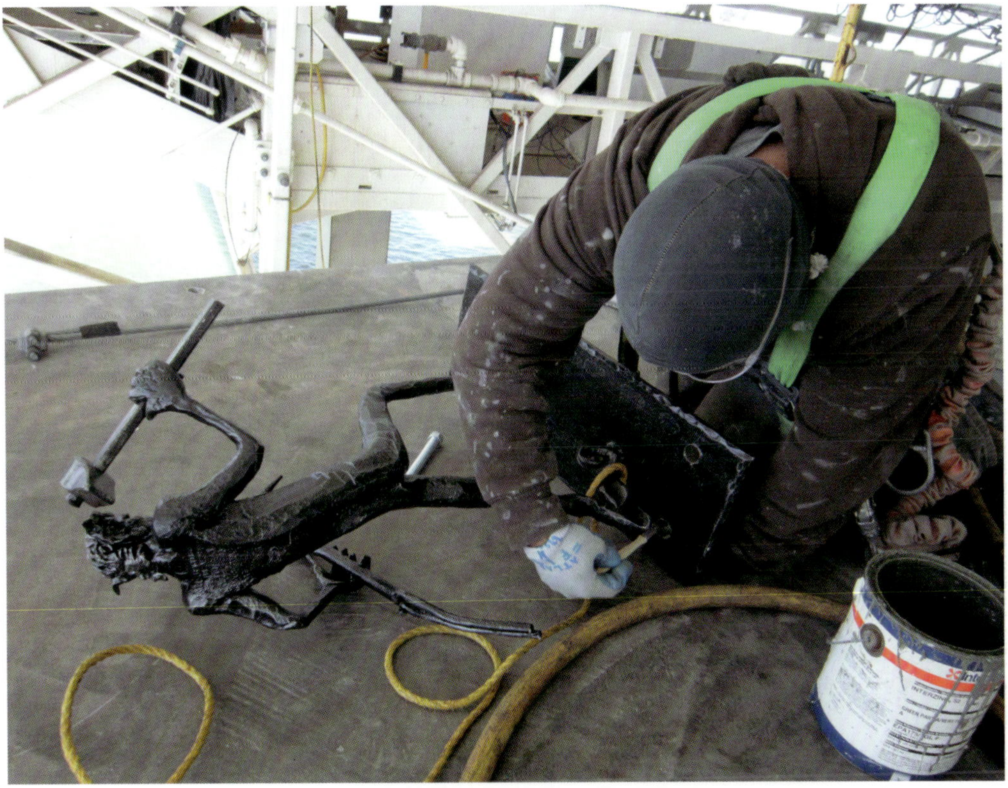

Right: By 11 a.m. of May 9, 2014, the troll was in the air being prepared for permanent residence at the top of the concrete pier of the east anchorage. From the pedestrian walkway, its basically under where the main cable passes through the road deck. (Courtesy of James Sturgeon.)

Below: Here iron worker Jim Benninghove works to install the new troll for long-term duty. (Courtesy of James Sturgeon.)

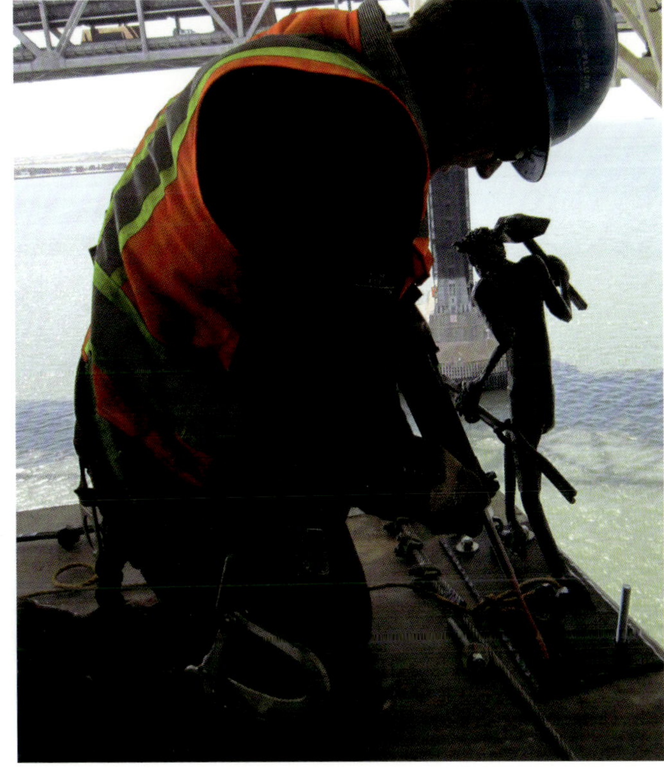

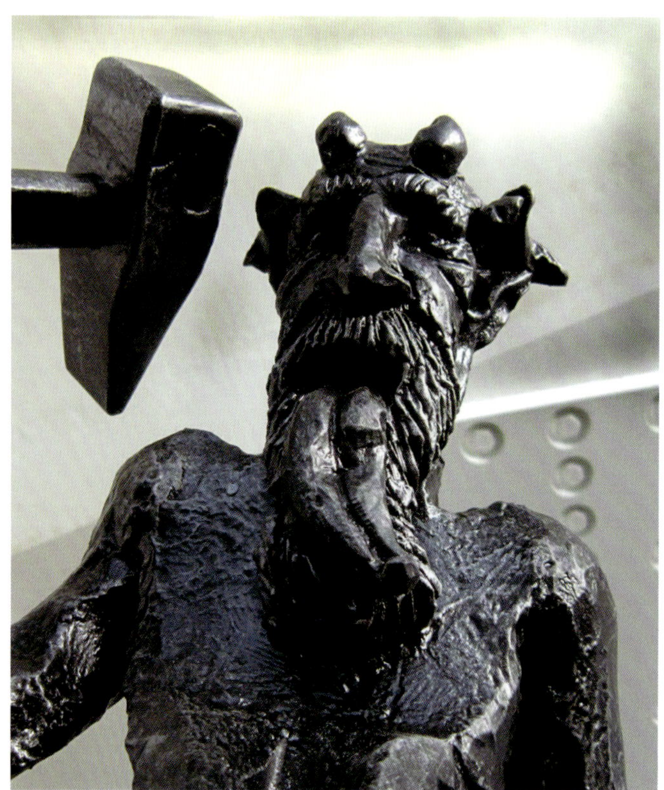

Left: The morning the new troll was installed, a series of detailed photographs were taken of the new troll's features. Like the old troll, Junior has a protruding tongue, horns, and is wielding traditional iron worker tools, a sledgehammer and oxyacetylene torch. (Courtesy of James Sturgeon.)

Below: The new troll, Junior, at his duty station, on the southwest corner. He appears hostile to the old bridge. (Courtesy of James Sturgeon.)

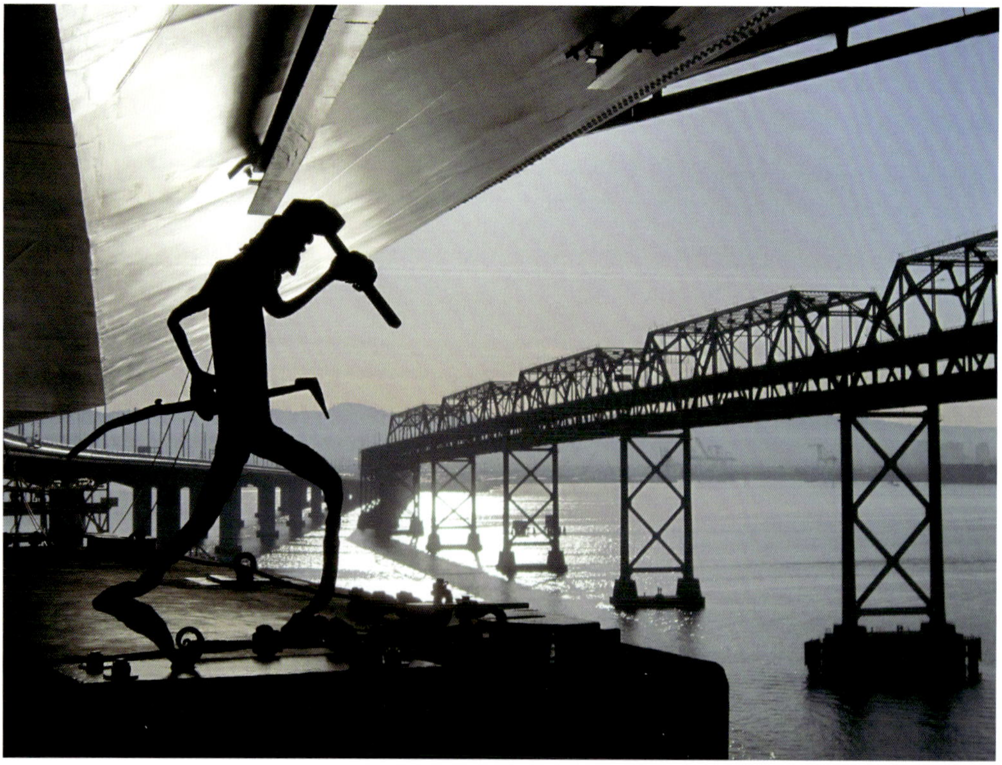

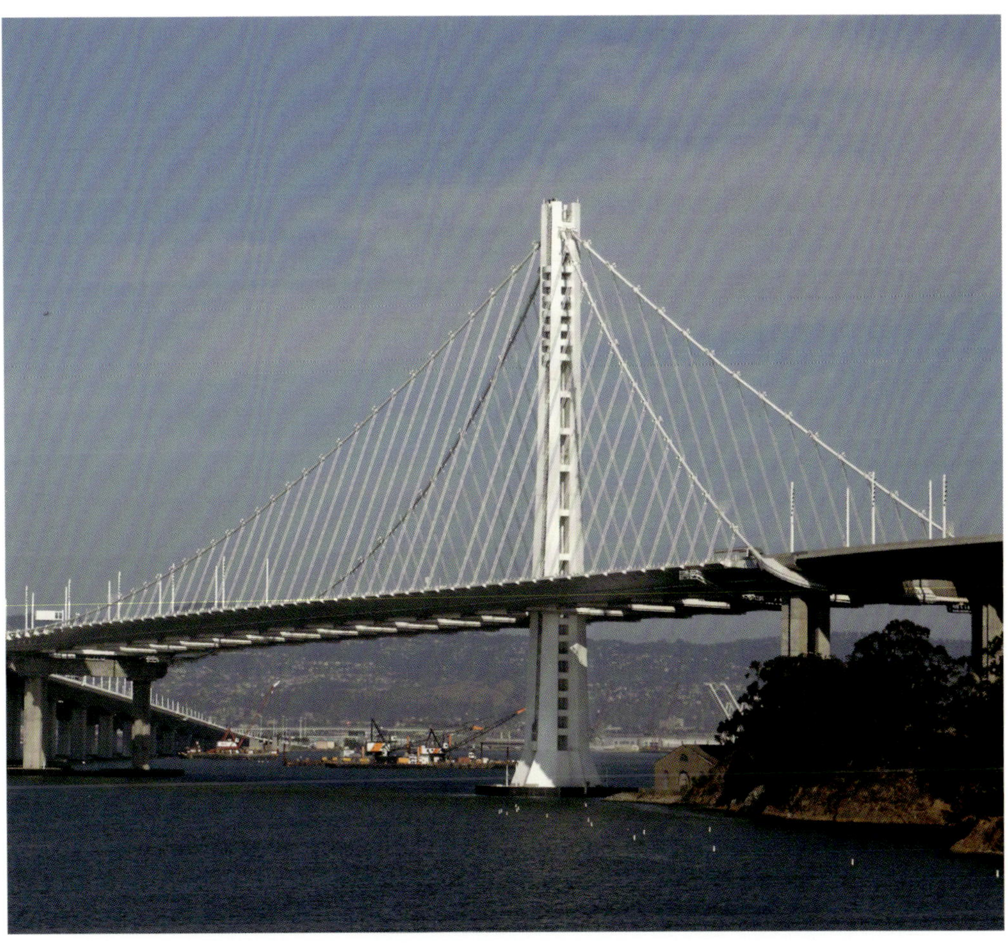

By 2017, the eastern span of the old Bay Bridge is just a memory. This photograph taken from Treasure Island in July 2017 looks east towards the elegant new span. Impressive in daylight, its true beauty is fully realized after dark when it is illuminated from above and below. (Photograph by John V. Robinson.)

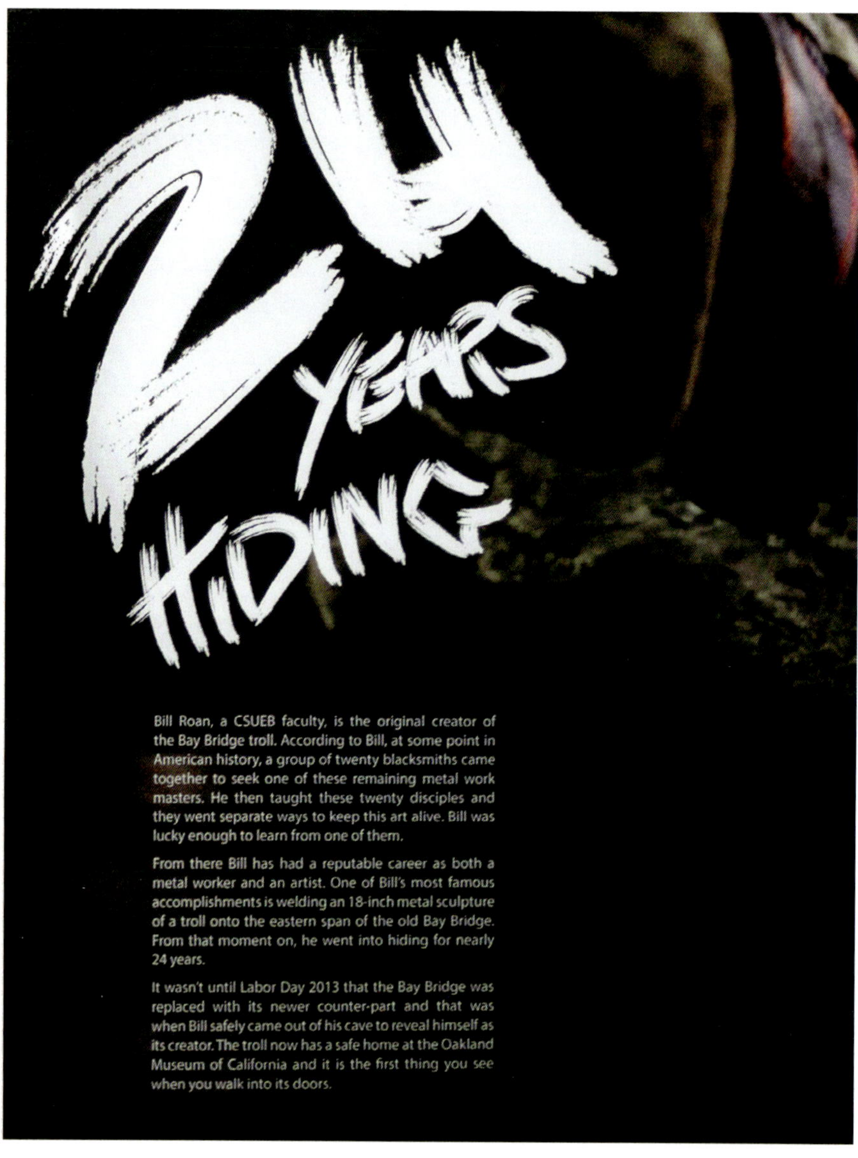

24 YEARS HIDING

Bill Roan, a CSUEB faculty, is the original creator of the Bay Bridge troll. According to Bill, at some point in American history, a group of twenty blacksmiths came together to seek one of these remaining metal work masters. He then taught these twenty disciples and they went separate ways to keep this art alive. Bill was lucky enough to learn from one of them.

From there Bill has had a reputable career as both a metal worker and an artist. One of Bill's most famous accomplishments is welding an 18-inch metal sculpture of a troll onto the eastern span of the old Bay Bridge. From that moment on, he went into hiding for nearly 24 years.

It wasn't until Labor Day 2013 that the Bay Bridge was replaced with its newer counter-part and that was when Bill safely came out of his cave to reveal himself as its creator. The troll now has a safe home at the Oakland Museum of California and it is the first thing you see when you walk into its doors.

Martin Hoang, a student at CSU East Bay, somehow ran across the story of the troll and traced it to Bill Roan, who happens to work at CSU East Bay. Looking for an interesting subject to photograph, Hoang contacted Roan, which led to an interesting collection of photographs of Bill Roan at work in the university's blacksmith shop. Martin Hoang's beautiful photographs were recognized in 2016 as an "Adobe Design Achievement Awards Finalist." His story and some of his photographs were also published, along with other talented artists from the school, in a handsome glossy 2017 magazine *Pioneer Edition.* (Author's collection.)

5

FINDING THE BAY BRIDGE TROLL

The working title of this project initially was "Finding the Bay Bridge Troll." For over twenty years I'd been aware of the little metal sculpture attached to the old Bay Bridge (demolished in 2017). And since I'd known where it was all along, I wasn't really looking for it. As I mentioned earlier, as the new bridge was being finished, there was renewed interest in Bay Bridge Troll's fate. Some of that interest was simple confirmation, "is there really such a thing as a Bay Bridge Troll?"

I began wondering about the troll. Were there other bridge trolls? Were there equivalent things in labor culture? Well, yes. Our Bay Bridge Trolls are interesting examples of the juxtaposition between craft and art. Many artists use craft skills in their creations and many people who work with craft tools also find the need to express themselves creatively. Muffler men are a good example of this impulse. Muffler shops in California often create sculptures, called muffler men, welded together from mufflers, old catalectic convertors, and exhaust pipes to create trade signs for their shops to attract attention and hopefully business. Tin Smiths have also been known to create "tin men" out of ducts and sheet metal as trade signs to advertise their business. (I have no doubt that L. Frank Baum, the creator of the Tin Woodsman in the *Wizard of Oz* [1900], was inspired by a tin shop's trade sign.) Such creations, muffler men and tin men, often become local landmarks, as well as targets for vandals and pranksters. Some become prized examples of folk art and end up in museums, art galleries, and private collections. Such creations, aside from being useful advertising, are also opportunities for craftspeople to satisfy a creative impulse as well as publicly show off their craft skills. I guess chainsaw art would fall into this general category as well, since most people wouldn't associate chainsaws with artistic instruments unless they were already familiar with them for more practical work.

Academic books have been published on some of these topics: *Muffler Men* (2000) and *Tin Men* (2002) for example. I imagine books about chainsaw art have been published, but I don't know if they treat the subject as an intersection between work and art.

The Bay Bridge Trolls were created from a similar impulse: craft pride, artistic impulse, and the desire to demonstrate craft skills. But, unlike muffler men and tin men, the audience for the trolls was never the public at large. The trolls were created to show respect and pay homage to the many anonymous men and woman who design, build, and maintain our great bridges.

It is a custom in the building trades that goes back centuries to acknowledge completion of their work with a celebration. Among modern construction workers, this is known as a "topping out" ceremony. Since ironworkers are seldom involved in demolition or repair work, this job required something else to celebrate the achievement. Bill Roan's troll fit the bill nicely.

But after twenty-four years of relative obscurity, it suddenly became a local *cause celeb*. I started hearing questions and comments about a "so-called Bay Bridge Troll." I received emailed questions from interested people. In April 2013, I spoke with Megan McHugh, a documentary filmmaker who had heard about the little troll and seen my name associated with it. I gave her names and contact information of people I thought she should interview for her film. I did a phone interview with the *Los Angeles Times*. In September 2013, I spoke with Joe Rodriguez at *The San Francisco Bay Guardian* and shared my

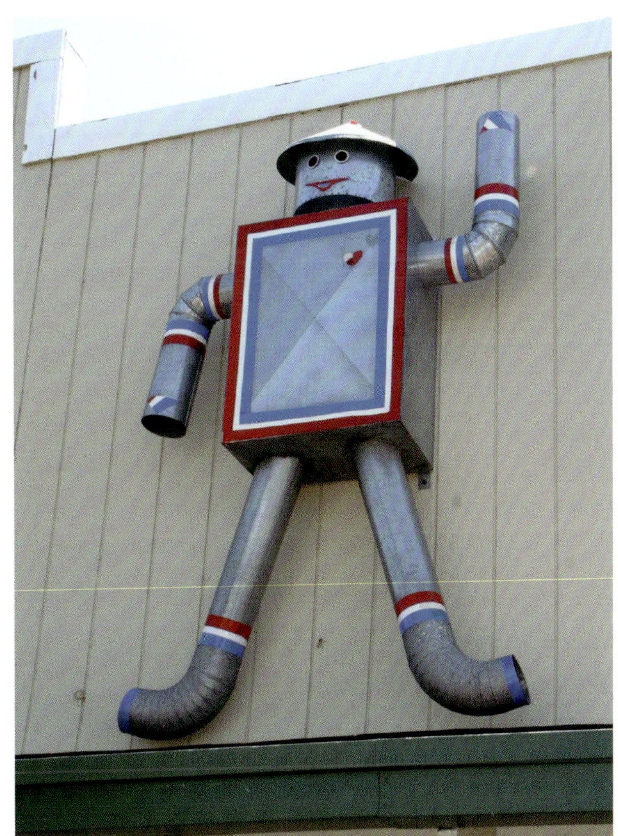

This 6-foot tin man adorns the roof of Angels Sheet Metal Inc. in Angels Camp, California. It is a fine example of a modern trade sign tradition juxtaposing craft skills with an artistic impulse. (Photograph by John V. Robinson.)

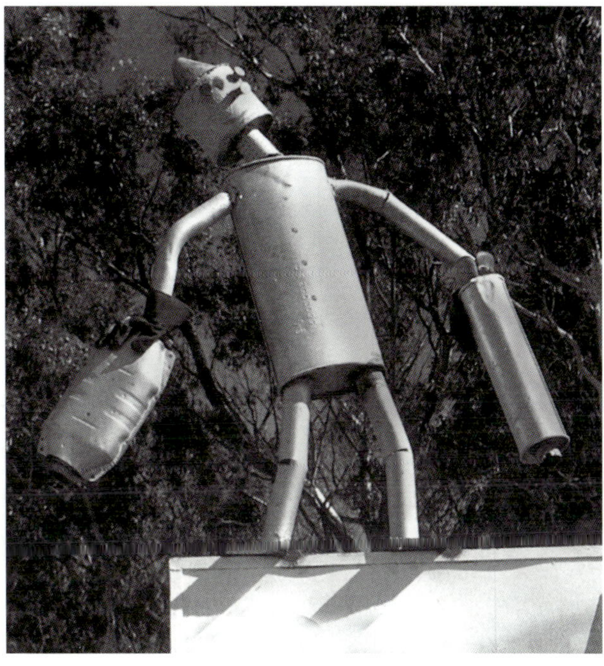

A good example of a muffler man on the roof of an auto repair shop in Southern California. (Author's collection.)

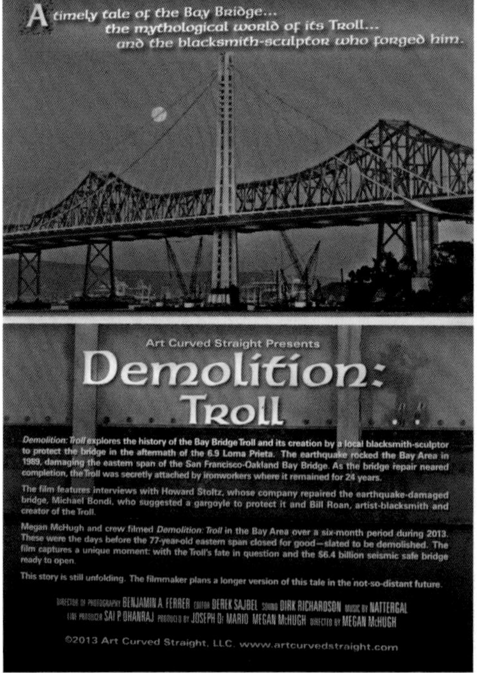

In 2013, Megan McHugh and Art Curved Straight Productions produced a ten-minute documentary on the Bay Bridge Troll. It premiered in November 2013 at the Scary Cow Independent Film Festival at the Castro Theater in San Francisco. The film's poster has a nice photograph of the old and new bridges that hosted the old and new trolls. (Courtesy of Art Curved Straight Production.)

long-standing interest in the troll. Most of this interest I had expected, and I encouraged it where I could. Then I started finding the Bay Bridge Troll in more personal and unexpected places.

On Saturday, November 2, 2013, the short documentary film titled *Demolition: Troll* premiered at the *Scary Cow Independent Film Festival at the* Castro Theater in San Francisco. I attended the showing of *Demolition: Troll,* with my daughter, Kathy. Bill Roan attended with his wife and some friends. It was a fun ten-minute tribute to the troll's story. I was happy to see Bill and his creation get some public acclaim after nearly a quarter-century of obscurity. I still hadn't decided to write about the troll so my interest was mostly personal curiosity. After the film, Kathy and I headed back to Crockett. Bill Roan and his party went across the street to get coffee at a local café. While chatting about the film, another customer, Matt Janulewicz, overhearing the subject of the conversation, approached the group and asked about the troll. Janulewicz had a tattoo of the trolls on his left arm and proceeded to show it to Bill and his friends. Roan got Janulewicz's contact information and snapped a couple of photos with his smartphone.

When Roan got back to his Oakland home, he emailed me about the encounter and sent me a photo of the tattoo and Matt's contact information. I didn't contact Matt until I was starting this project a couple of years later. On Sunday, April 23, 2017, I drove to San Francisco to meet Matt Janulewicz, see his tattoo that depicts both the old and new Bay Bridge Trolls, and listen to his story.

In 2007, Matt and his wife moved to the Bay Area from Southern California to take a job with Lucas Films. As a transplant to the area, Matt spent some time exploring. He had a bare arm that he wanted to get tattooed so he decided to get a sleeve with some of his favorite San Francisco icons: Sutro Tower, built in 1973, the 977-foot orange and white transmission tower that overlooks the city, a bison from the Golden Gate Park herd established in 1892, an image of Yoda from Star Wars at the fountain near Lucas Films headquarters in the Presidio, the Coca Cola billboard at Bryant and 5th Street, and one of the historic F-line streetcars. Above his elbow and covering much of his bicep and triceps are tattoos of the old and new Bay Bridge Trolls with the tower of the new Bay Bridge in the background. Matt is tall with long arms, so there is plenty of room for such an intricate tattoo.

I found it a curious assortment of images. I couldn't help but notice the obvious choices, like the Golden Gate Bridge, Coit Tower, cable cars, the Ferry building's clock tower, and the Pyramid Building, were missing from the tattoo. I wondered why. Matt told me, "Well, It was a job with Lucas Films that brought me and my wife to the city, so that accounts for Yoda. I just like bison. They have a small herd of bison in Golden Gate Park. People drive past the 'Coca Cola Billboard' every day. But how many people really notice it? We tend to look past advertising without really acknowledging it. It's a really cool sign." Why the Sutro Tower and the F-line car? "They are both visually interesting parts of the city."

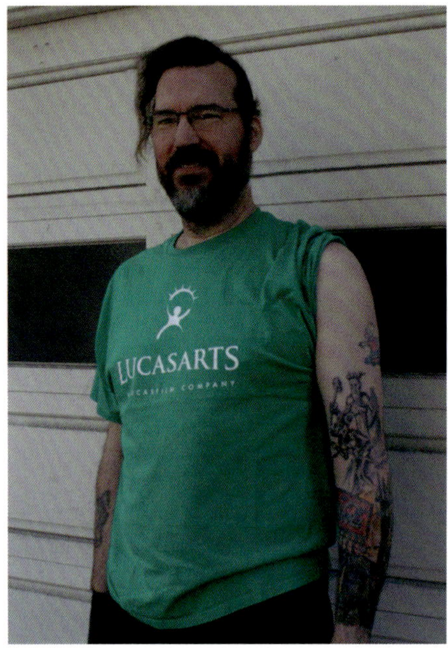

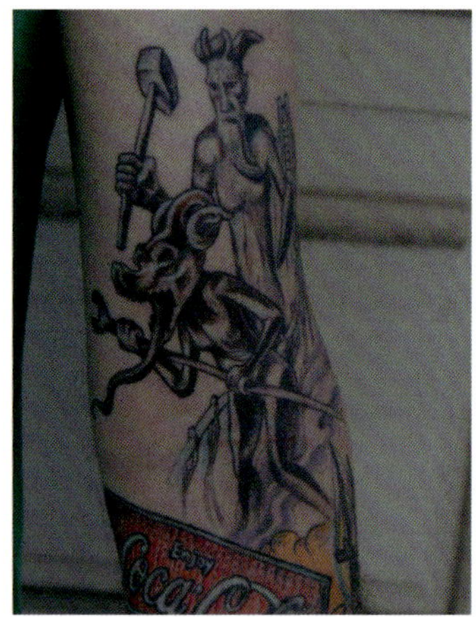

Pictured here from 2017 is Matt Janulewicz and his tattoo sleeve depicting some lesser-known San Francisco icons and featuring the old and new Bay Bridge Trolls. (Photograph by John V. Robinson.)

But the Bay Bridge Troll! That was truly a head scratcher. After all, to inscribe something on your body permanently, the thing must have some personal meaning to you. (At least, so I thought as a man with no tattoos.) Matt told me that the old troll seemed a very San Francisco thing. "Where else would you find a work of art, created after a catastrophe, and then placed where it can't be seen for nearly twenty-five years? So, when I heard about the new troll I thought, I'll use that too. The two trolls really lend themselves to good tattoo."

"I was in a coffee shop on day and I overheard some people talking at another table. They mentioned something about the Bay Bridge Troll and I approached them to join the conversation and show them my tattoos. Well it turns out one of the guys there was Bill Roan, who made the old troll. They had been to see a short documentary film about the old troll. I think they thought I had been at the film too. But I hadn't, it was just pure chance that we met. Bill took some snapshots of my tattoo with his phone, I gave him my email address, and we parted. I didn't really think about it again until I got my first email from you."

When I did my preliminary research about the Bay Bridge Troll, I did what anyone in the year 2017 would do: I googled "Bay Bridge Troll" just to see how far, if any, the little troll had penetrated into pop culture. There was not much there that I didn't already know. Then I found a photo on the website Flickr that showed the troll on a belt buckle. It was uploaded by Aimee Brooks, a photographer and bridge aficionado from Halifax, Nova Scotia. Aimee graciously allowed me to publish her photograph, and told me via email that she had created the buckle, "in 2011 for a friend of mine who lives in the Bay Area, he was working on a costume inspired by the Bay Bridge, and we did a trade, he sent me a couple of ornaments from the Golden Gate Bridge gift shop (I'm in Canada and they wouldn't ship outside the US), and in return I made the belt for him, including the buckle. My friend is a huge San Francisco fan, he's done lots of artwork inspired by the city, so he knew about the troll and loved the idea of working it into the costume. The belt itself is patterned after the bridge's trusses. I, too, am an architecture and bridge enthusiast, and learned about the troll while researching the Bay Bridge."

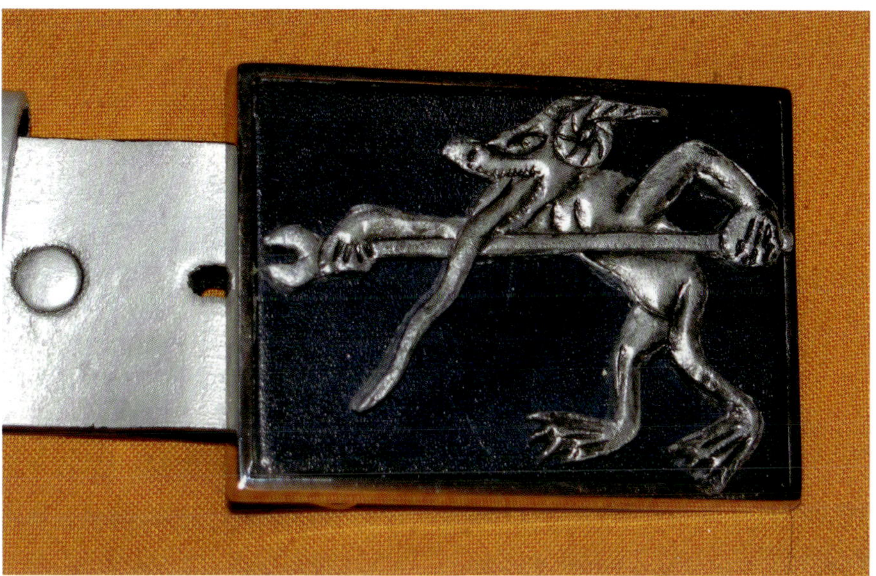

Where does the Bay Bridge Troll live?

Ask

www.ask.com

The idea of the Bay Bridge Troll became the tease of an ASK.com advertisement. In 2013, a large billboard with the question, "Where does the Bay Bridge Troll live?" appeared for a few months on the San Francisco side of the bridge. (Courtesy of ASK.com.)

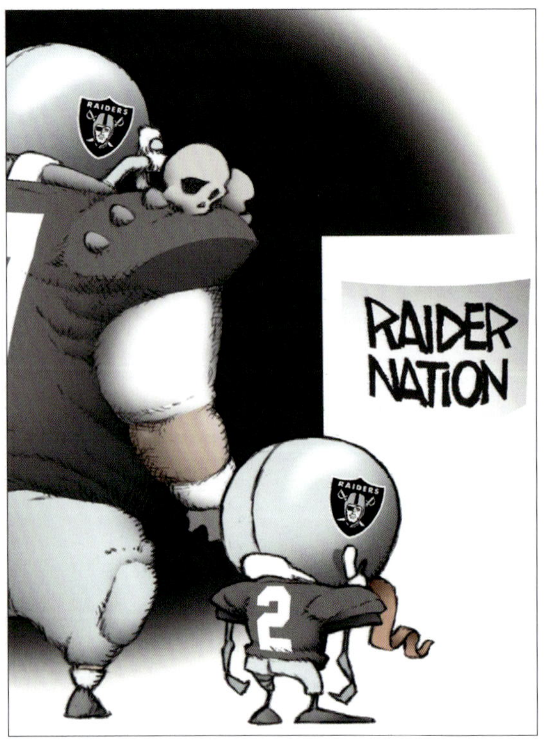

Political cartoonist Tom Meyers featured the troll in a three-panel cartoon titled "The Old Bay Bridge Troll Looks for a New Job." (I separated the panels for better presentation in this format.) Panel one shows the troll in Raider's gear heading into the stadium with a Raider Nation sign ahead of him, perhaps suggesting the troll as a fitting mascot for the Oakland Raider's football team or a member of the notorious "Black Hole" fan group. (Courtesy Tom Meyers.)

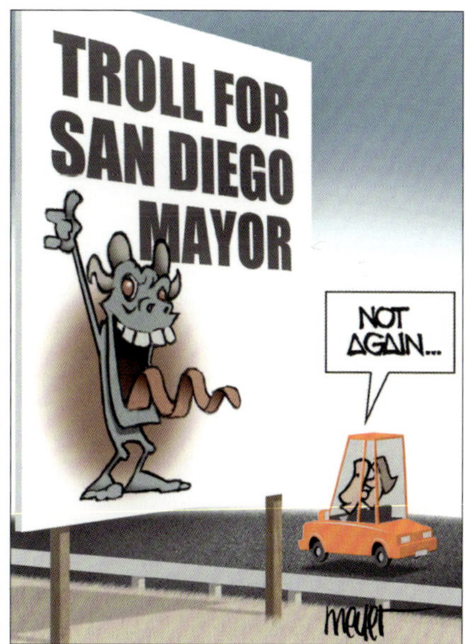

The second panel has a couple in a car lamenting a "Troll for San Diego Mayor" billboard, alluding to disgraced San Diego Mayor, Bob Filner, who resigned from office in 2013 due to numerous sexual harassment charges. (Courtesy Tom Meyers.)

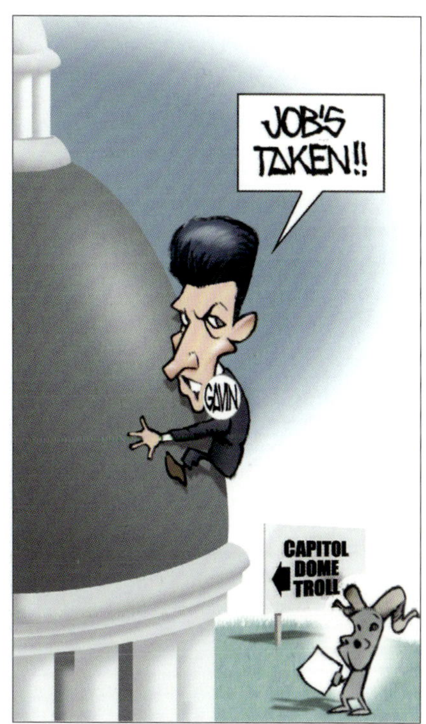

The third panel in the sequence shows, former San Francisco Mayor and current Lt. Governor, Gavin Newsome, clinging to the Capitol dome, proclaiming "Job's taken" while the old troll looks on. (Courtesy Tom Meyers.)

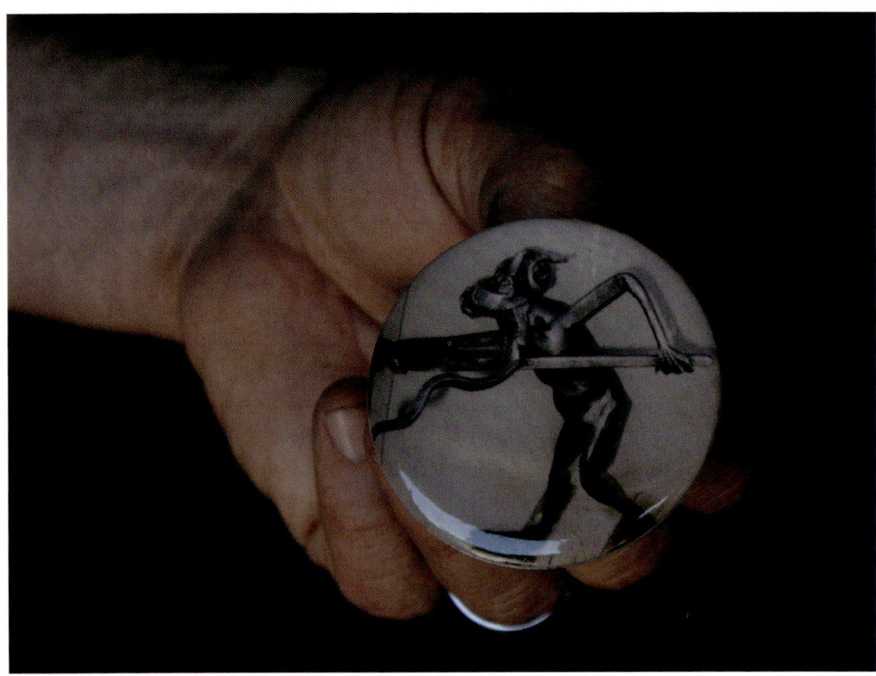

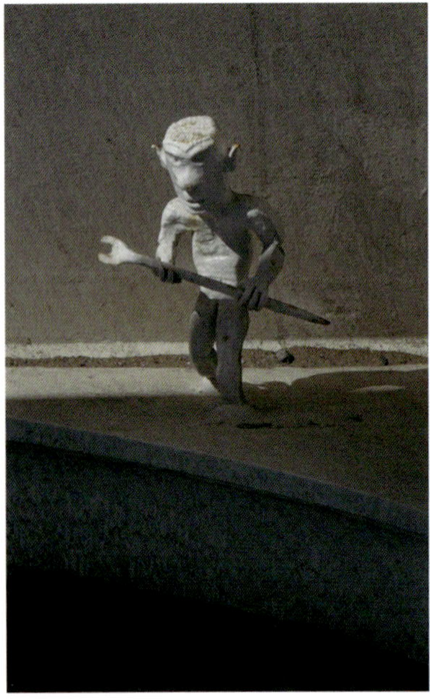

Above: Some local entrepreneur made buttons with the old troll on them. Whether they were for sale or merely souvenirs given to a lucky few, I do not know. I imagine they will achieve collectable status. (Photograph by John V. Robinson.)

Left: At a recent event for the Pinole Historical Society, someone asked me, "How many trolls are there?" "Well," came my reply, "It depends on what counts as a troll. There is: the old troll (1989), the 'twin troll' in the lobby of Rigging International's Alameda office (also made by Bill Roan immediately after the quake of 1989), the new troll (2013) in place now, and this little guy. Visible from pedestrian walkway, he is about twelve inches high and holding a spud-wrench at high port, ready to fend off any hazards to the new bridge. I suspect he was placed there surreptitiously by bridge workers. I don't know if Caltrans knows, or approves of its placement, so I won't reveal its specific location on the bridge." (Photograph by John V. Robinson.)

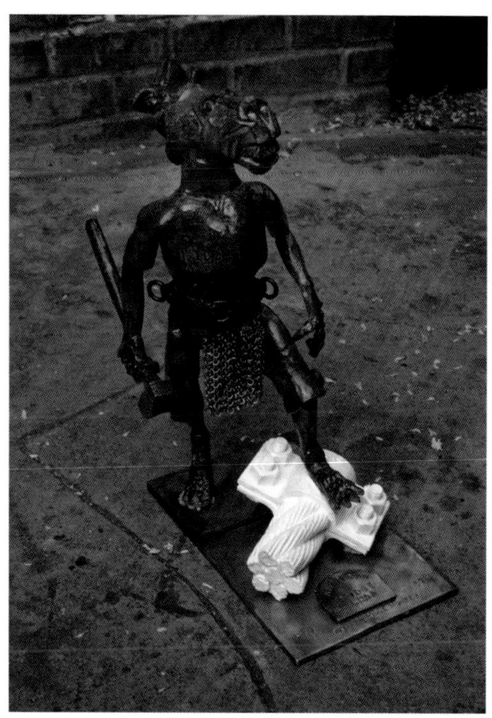

In anticipation of a new troll for the new bridge, Bill Roan created a mascot for the new bridge. In April 2013, Bill Roan invited me to his Oakland home to show me the "Bridge Monkey." The old-time bridge men were sometimes called "Bridge Monkeys." I think he hoped someone would smuggle it onto the new bridge. A plan was suggested to attach the Bridge Monkey to the very top of the new bridge's tower. That plan did not come to fruition. But it may still one day. So, it seems, there were several competing schemes to re-troll the new bridge. (Photograph by John V. Robinson.)

In early 2017 I received an email from Krista Dossetti, editor of *Cal State East Bay*, the alumni magazine, asking about the Bay Bridge Troll. She alerted me to Martin Hoang (Class of 2016), a photographer who done an award-winning project about Bill Roan and the Bay Bridge Troll. I contacted Martin and he shared his knowledge of the troll and graciously shared a few photographs of his photo project featuring Bill Roan.

Martin Hoang:

It's crazy how I heard about the Bay Bridge Troll. Bill was a living legend to me. I first heard about the troll when I was in 5th grade. My teacher mentioned to the class that there is an 18-inch troll protecting the bridge and we should look for it if we ever crossed the Bay Bridge. I never found it.

But almost ten years after, I sat next to Bill Roan in Basics of New Media class. I never knew what he looked like, nor who created the troll. Bill would subtly drop hints in class about his fascinations for trolls and he dropped the biggest hint when he illustrated the troll for our final project in class. During that same weekend, I went to the Oakland museum with a buddy who needed to look at art for his class assignment. To my amazement the first thing that greeted me was Bill's bridge troll. The rest, as they say, was history.

I asked Bill if I could photograph him recreating the bridge troll's head for my class assignment. From there I took the photos and sent it off to the Adobe Design Achievement Awards the next year and was selected as a finalist in the commercial photography category. If you didn't know, the Adobe Design Achievement Awards is the biggest and most premiere student competition there is. With over 5,300 entries worldwide the chances of being a finalist or winning is 0.01%. You are more likely to be accepted into Harvard than be given an honor in this award.

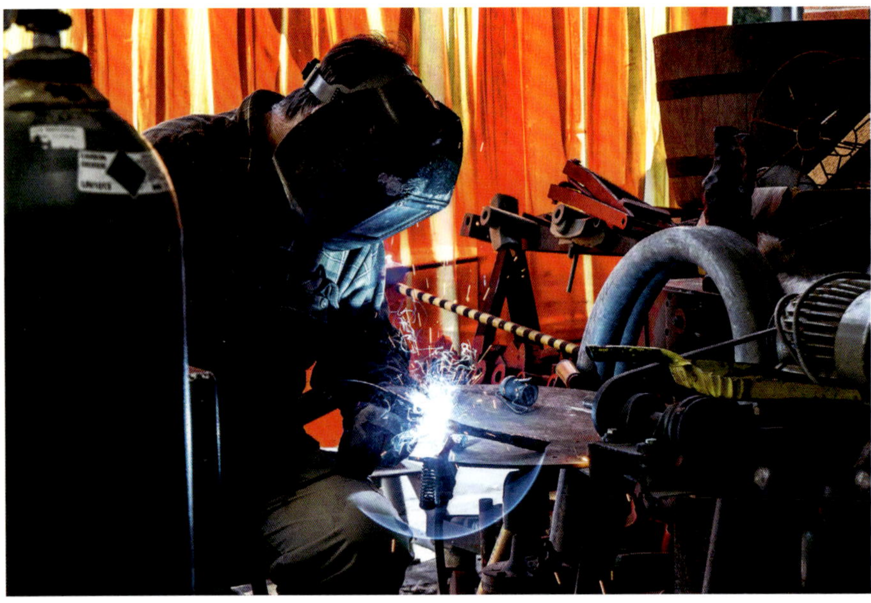

Bill Roan at work in the CSU East Bay metal shop and weld bay. (Photograph by Martin Hoang.)

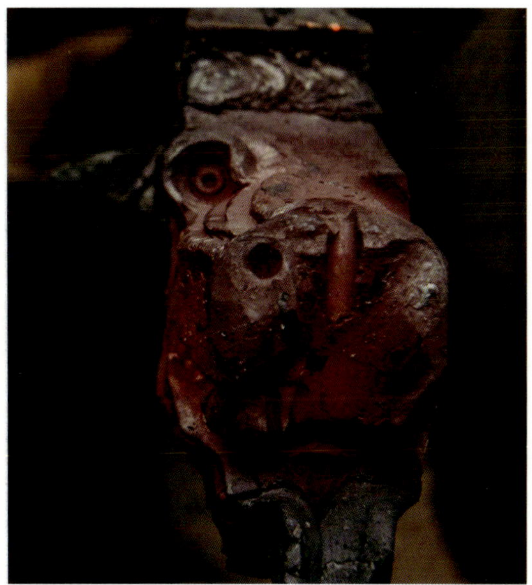

A close-up of a partially completed troll face recreated by Roan for Martin Hoang's award-winning photography project. (Photograph by Martin Hoang.)

Now, to circle back to the beginning of the story. The working title of the manuscript was *Finding the Bay Bridge Troll.* While writing this short book I interviewed the people involved in the creation, installation and removal of both the old and new trolls. I talked to, and corresponded with, various people who embraced the troll as an important part of San Francisco Bay Area culture and lore. It has been twenty-seven years since the troll was first installed on the old bridge. During those years I'd known about the troll, I'd gathered information about the troll, I'd written about the troll, but I had never actually seen the Bay Bridge Troll. I had several missed connections. When it was down at the Oakland Museum, for various personal reasons, I could not get time to see it. When it showed up at the 2013 bridge opening ceremony, I could not wrangle an invite to the opening; but, then again, the troll's appearance was a bit of a surprise. As this project drew to its conclusion, I decided that if I ever was going to meet the troll, the time was now. I certainly had a motivation. It would make a fitting end to this book.

After a few false leads, I called John Huseby, a photographer who works for Caltrans. Did he, by any chance, know where the old troll was kept? Yes, it turns out, the troll was in a hallway, off the lobby, of the Caltrans District 4 office in downtown Oakland. It was on display with construction photographs and other bits and pieces of bridge memorabilia. The following Monday, I drove down to see the troll and take a few preliminary snapshots. As I walked around the District 4 lobby looking for the troll, I paused to look at photographs of the Alfred Zampa Memorial Bridge, the Benicia Martinez Bridge, and the new Bay Bridge that adorn the walls. These photographs, taken by Caltrans photographers William Hall and John Huseby, brought back a flood of memories of the time I had spent photographing these bridges. The little troll was mounted on a beam and kept in a Plexiglas case. The light was poor, and a flash would reflect off the case. (Not an easy shot.) I thought of the best angle for the photo in this crowded, poorly lit corridor and knew I would need help. So, the next afternoon, I drove back down to Oakland with my camera and my son, Kyle. I posed with the little troll while Kyle snapped the photographs. Success at last.

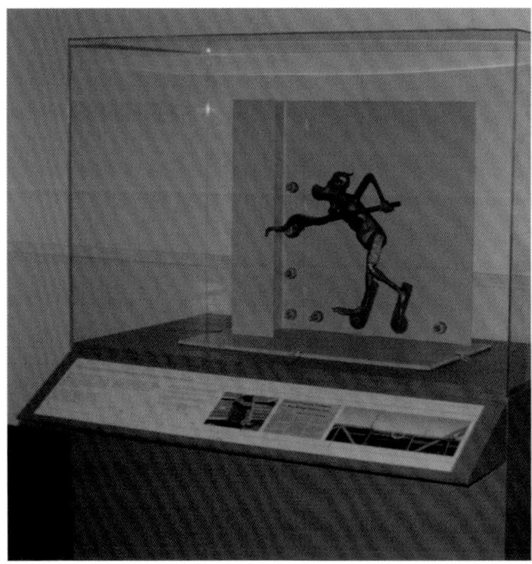

Bay Bridge Troll under glass at Caltrans District 4 office in Oakland. (Photograph by Kyle L. Robinson.)

The Fremont Street Troll is only obliquely related to our story. I have, in my investigation, been told that people, when asked, claim the Bay Bridge Troll is 18 feet high, or even forty feet tall. I suspect people are confusing our little troll, which is hidden from view, with the much larger Fremont Street Troll which is in plain sight for all to see, climb on, and photograph.

Which leads me to my final thought in this book on the subject of bridges and trolls. Where are the other bridge trolls? Are there other bridge trolls around the country? If any reader of this book knows of other bridge trolls, please feel free to contact the author at jvrobins@aol.com with the particulars.

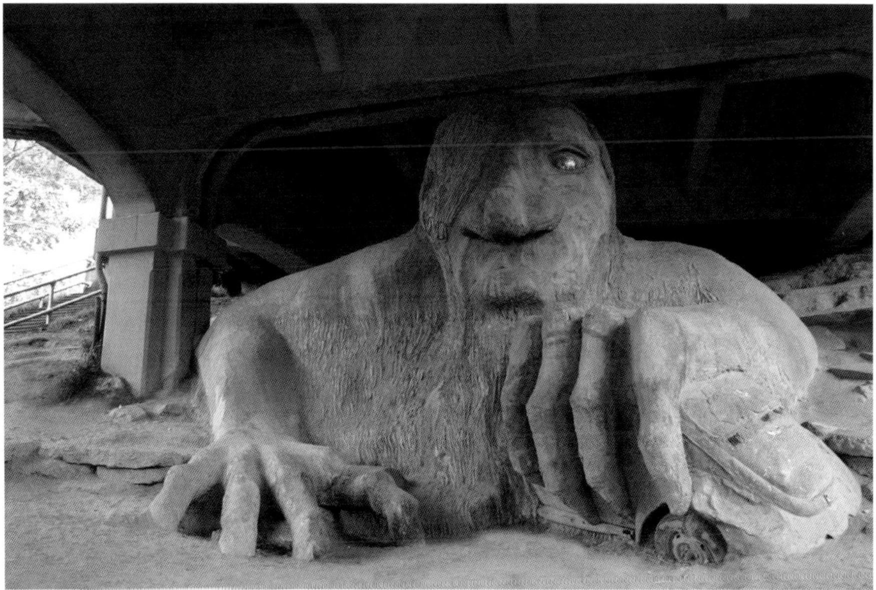

Where are the other trolls? There is at least one other well-known bridge troll in the United States. In Seattle, Washington, exists the Fremont Street Troll. Published accounts state that in 1989, Seattle asked the *Fremont Arts Council* to hold an art competition to rehabilitate the area under the bridge, which was becoming a dumping ground and haven for drug dealers and the homeless. A team led by sculptor Steve Badanes won the competition and created this massive troll. The Fremont Street Troll is 18 feet high and is made from steel rebar, wire, and two tons of concrete. One can get a sense for how big it is by the fact it is crushing a Volkswagen Beetle in his left hand. It has a shiny metal eye made from the hubcap of a car. Like our Bay Bridge Troll, the Fremont Street Troll was inspired by the *Three Billy Goats Gruff* story.

Bill Roan Was Here

[illegible] Message from [illegible] Caltrans

[illegible]cordi[illegible] the [illegible] is an unaccept[illegible] a[illegible]inati[illegible] th[illegible]y Br[illegible]. It scrutinize[illegible] safety o[illegible]os[illegible]wh[illegible]e [illegible]ve it[illegible] shou[illegible]moved [illegible]he[illegible]te[illegible] Wh[illegible]o yo[illegible]t's welded [illegible]hut? So yo[illegible]e[illegible]ing[illegible] we [illegible]e t[illegible]ove the[illegible]tire span in o[illegible] em[illegible] the [illegible]l?

I w[illegible] t[illegible]nd [illegible]chev[illegible] wise crackin[illegible]art guy that di[illegible]is[illegible]nd su[illegible]his pa[illegible]s off. I want him[illegible]ked up i[illegible] prison[illegible] as lo[illegible] a h[illegible]ve. This is a multi[illegible]on d[illegible]r screw up by some street a[illegible]st. This is v[illegible]ndalis[illegible] of public property and shou[illegible] no[illegible]e st[illegible]d for!

We Caltrans will ensure th[illegible]sa[illegible] those who utilizes our bridge and infr[illegible]u[illegible]es. We wi[illegible]ot stand to these hooligan ac[illegible]ns [illegible]d [illegible]ill [illegible]os[illegible]ute the individual or individuals involved with t[illegible]ons[illegible]se. In the meantime if you have any information on the person who did this, please contact your local authority."

Goodnight Bill Roan wherever you are.

APPENDIX I

PETITION TO THE GOVERNOR OF CALIFORNIA: JERRY BROWN

We the free and independent citizens of the Great State of California, demand the immediate release of a fellow citizen, known simply as the old Bay Bridge Troll, who was unjustly evicted from its home and deprived of its livelihood.

It was condemned not by a jury of its peers, but by a handful of bureaucrats, who used eminent domain to condemn and then confiscate its property.

Said Bridge Troll gained all rights to protect the citizens, commuters, bridge workers and law enforcement officers lawfully through squatter's rights of 1989. This indiscriminate incarceration by Caltrans at the highest level has deprived the troll of its freedom to roam the New Bridge Span at will, to make repairs as needed, and to have free association with its fellow bridge workers.

We, the undersigned, further demand an immediate accounting of the old Bay Bridge Troll's current whereabouts.

Name, County, State, Country of Origin

APPENDIX II

PHOTO GALLERY OF BILL ROAN'S METAL SCULPTURES

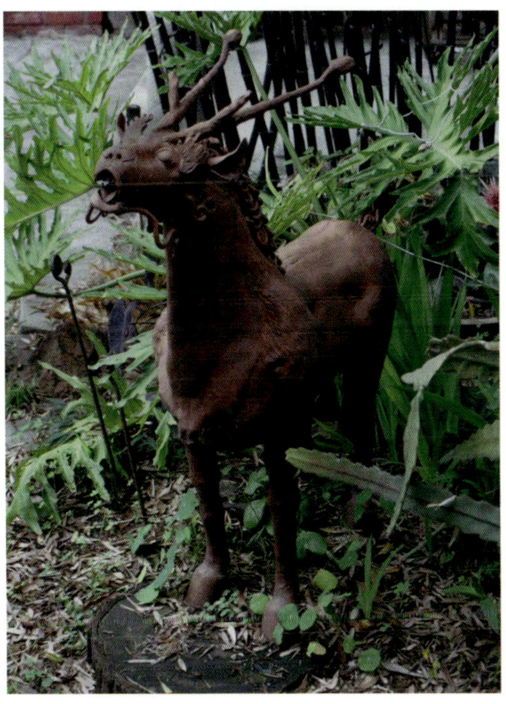

Karin, Chinese unicorn.
Forged steel and paint
43" x 53" x 12" wide

Asian Unicorn. Inspired after seeing my first bottle of Kiran Beer. Life size.
(Photograph by John V. Robinson.)

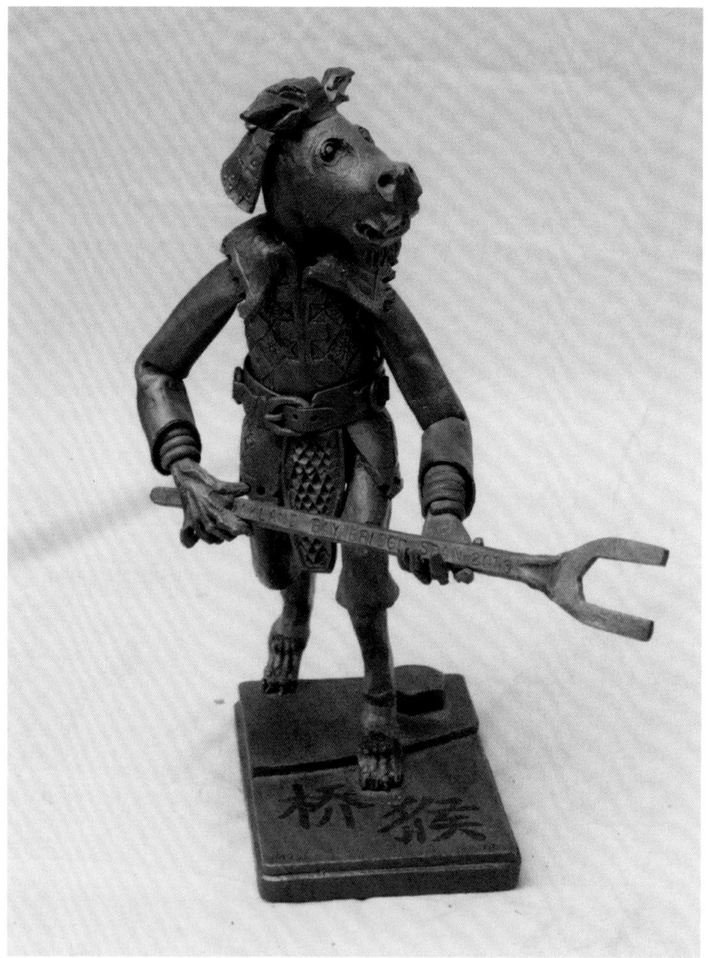

Chinese Bridge Monkey
Forged steel and copper paint
18" x 9" x 14"

Second Bay Bridge Monkey, part of artist's personal collection. Since the major steel structures that made up the new Bay Bridge were supplied by the Chinese, I created a second Chinese themed Bridge Monkey to honor their contribution to the project. To bring good luck to a bridge, a piece of the bridge must be incorporated into the sculpture. The bolt that holds the two pieces of bridge together is one of the bolts that were collected on site.

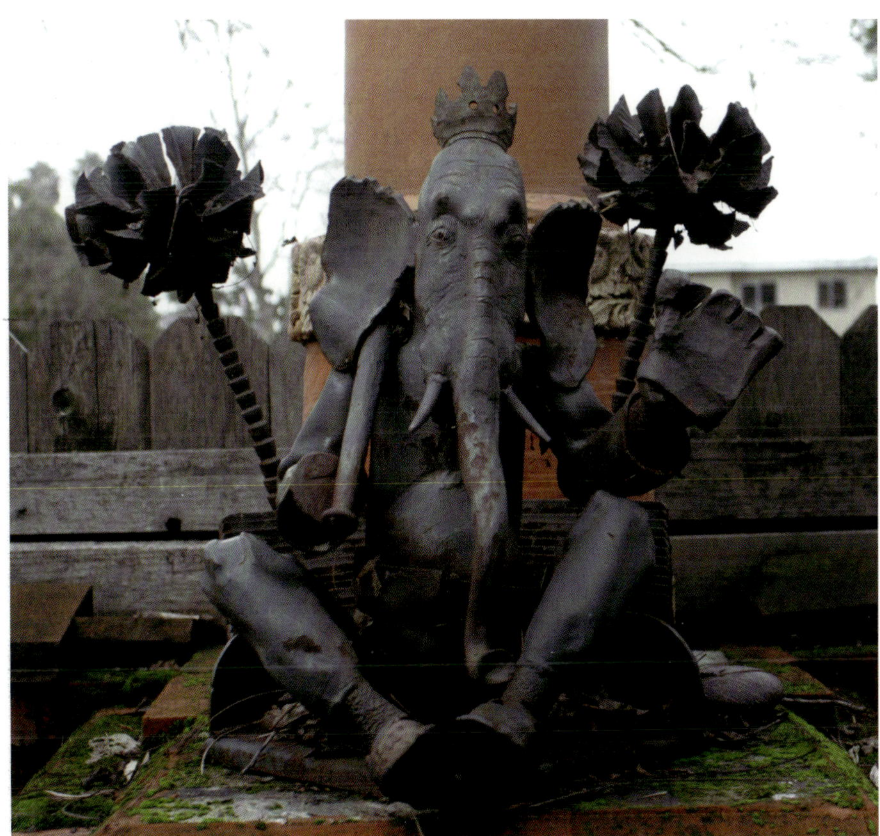

Baseball God
Forged steel and paint
20" x 17" x 21"

In 1989, the San Francisco Giants and Oakland A's were about to start the World Series when the earthquake disrupted the game. The A's would sweep the series and Giant's fans were talking about an earthquake curse. Since then the Giants have won several world championships and the A's have suffered from a Baseball curse. In their heyday the A's were unstoppable; they were like Baseball Gods. This sculpture was made in the image of the A's elephant mascot, to bring them good luck. Originally it was going to sit on a stand that would allow the batters to hang their bats from, to energize the wood for home runs. When offered to the A's, it was rejected because baseball players are so superstitious—what might be thought to be lucky for one player, might be thought to be a curse for another. Since then the sculpture has sat outside, rusting in its little stadium, much like the A's do today.

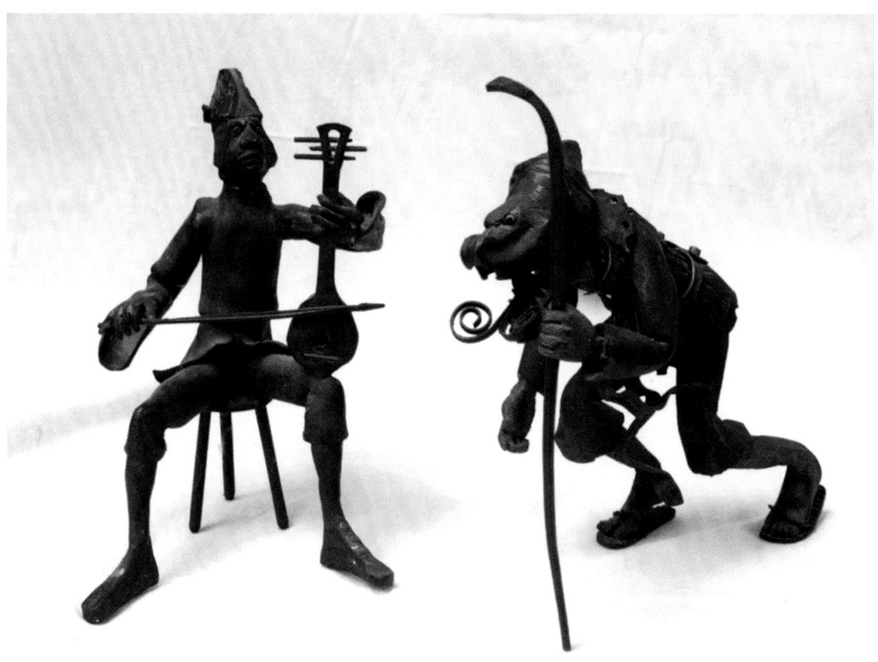

Ghost Dancer
Forged steel
14" x 9" x 10"

&

Dragon Dancer
Forged steel, stones, and paint
15" x 13" x 6"

The rich multi-cultural history of California was the inspiration for these two pieces. The hustle and bustle of San Francisco's Chinatown and Japantown, with their many antique shops and festivals, sparked my imagination: the Dragon Dancers on New Year's, an old man sitting on a corner playing a Chinese fiddle, the traditional festival costumes, and the crowds at the many markets and apothecaries. The city was filled with hidden treasures ripe for my imagination

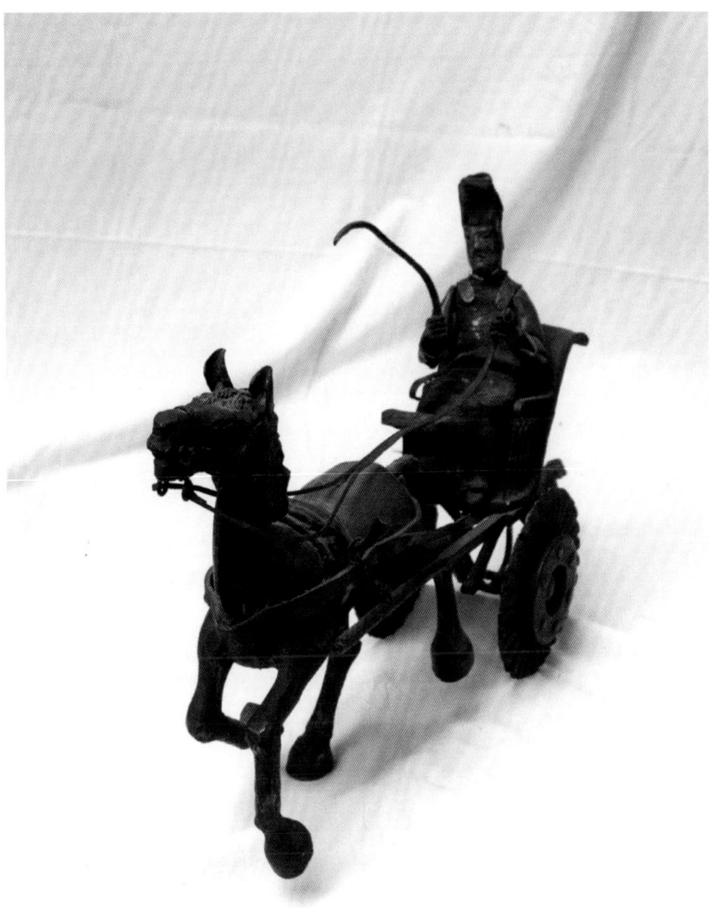

Pony cart
Forged steel
20" high x 28" long x 6" wide

Chinese Pony Cart, pull toy. As it is pulled along, the driver raises his arm to whip the horse to go faster.

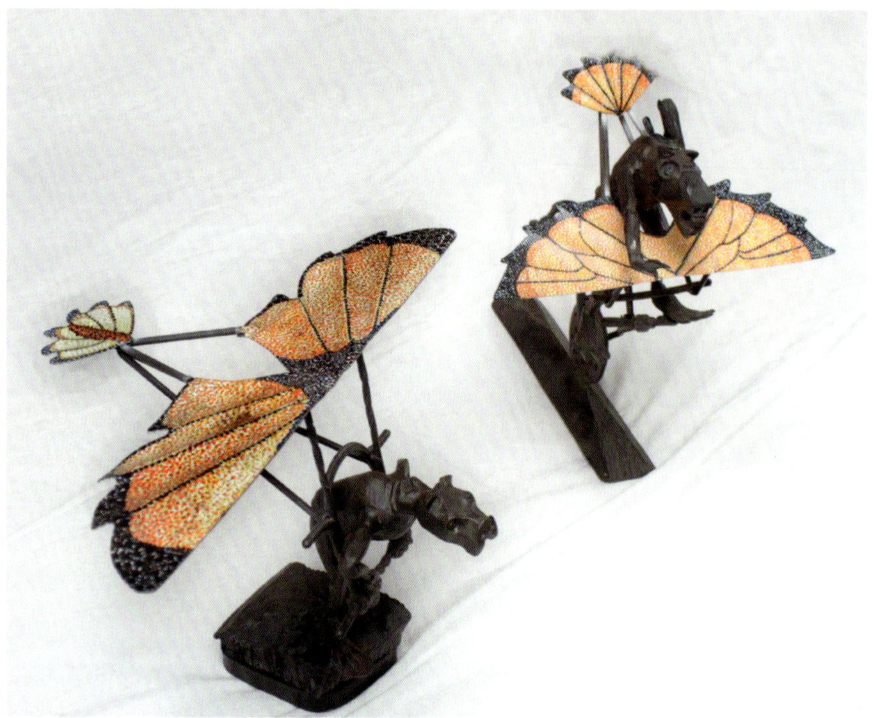

Butterfly Gliders
Forged steel, paint
13" x 10" x 12"

Butterfly Gliders, a series of sculptures inspired by the movie *Those Magnificent Men in Their Flying Machines.*

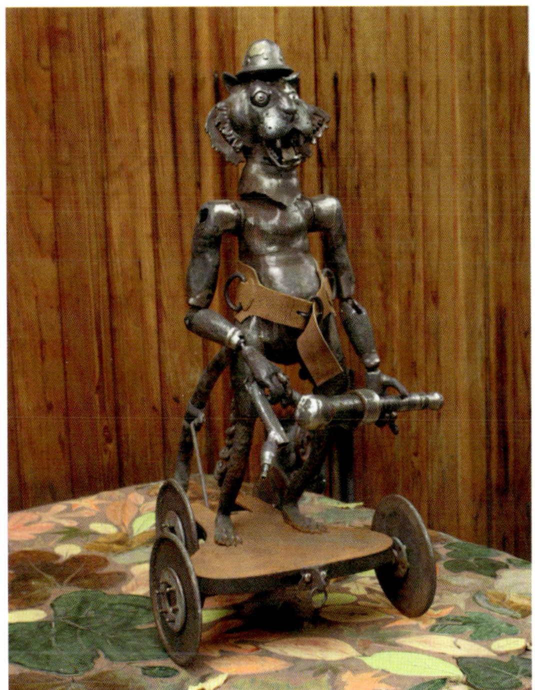

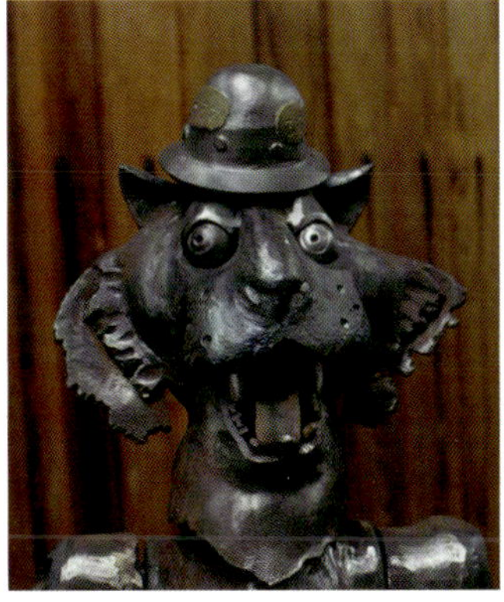

Bridge Cat
forged steel with leather belt
20" x 28" x 6"

Humans love their pets and there are several examples of feral animals showing up at job sites, only to be adopted by the workers. The Hoover Dam had a black dog and the 1958 Carquinez Bridge had the little dog Rags. I wondered if the original Bay Bridge might have had an animal mascot? So he made this bridge cat.

Detail of bridge cat head: Forged steel pull toy, eyes rotate in sockets, removable hard hat with iron workers union brass ID chips, leather utility belt with tie off loops, poseable arms with various interchangeable tools, tail moves up and down when pulled.

APPENDIX III

THE TWIN TROLL

As I mentioned earlier, Bill Roan created two trolls in 1989: the troll that was attached to the Bay Bridge as part of the overall repairs, and a twin troll that was made at the request of the principal contractor, Rigging International, that repaired the bridge. The twin troll was taken to the company office and mounted on a section of damaged steel that was removed from the bridge.

While I was preparing this manuscript for publication, I thought it would be a good idea to revisit the "twin troll" at the Alameda Office of Rigging International. I had last visited the twin troll in 2007.

A quick Google search informed me that Rigging International had been purchased by Sarens Group in 2009. The twin troll remined on duty at the Alameda office until 2013 when it was temporarily loaned to the Oakland Museum as part of an overall display about the Bay Bridge. In due course, Sarens Group closed the Alameda office, and its operations moved to Houston, Texas. Fair enough, but what about the twin troll?

I made a few phone calls to Susan Lavering and Shayrun Ali at Sarens USA and was surprised to find out the twin troll was missing. The first reports were that after hurricane Harvey tore through Texas in 2017, the Sarens' office, like much of Houston, was flooded and inaccessible for several days. When things calmed down, some personnel made their way back to the office to see what

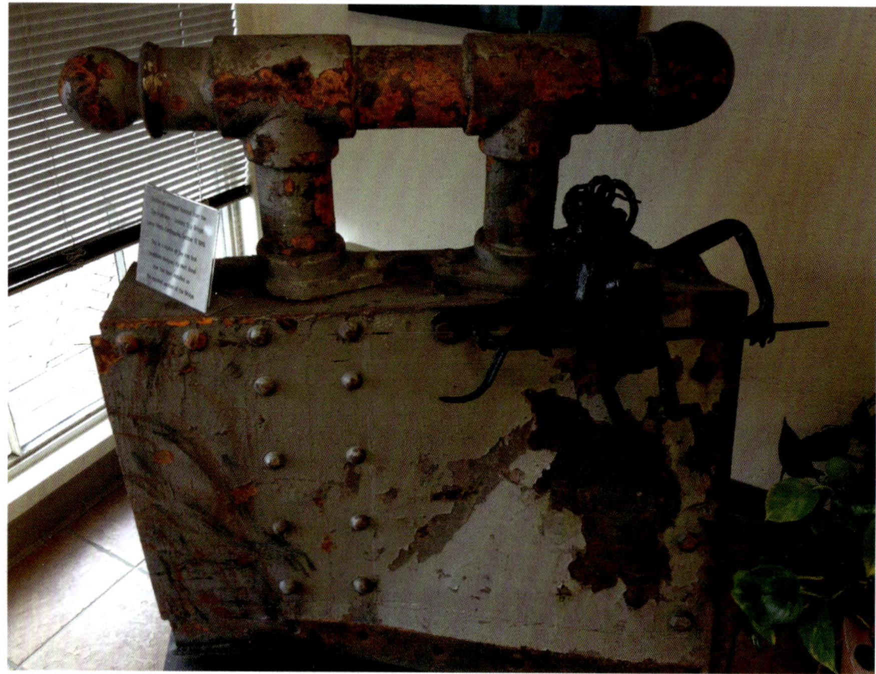

Twin Troll in the lobby Rigging International's Alameda office, 2010. (Photograph by John V. Robinson.)

was salvageable. To their surprise, the steel beam from the old bridge was in the lobby but the twin troll was gone!

The steel-beam was still there but the twin troll was gone. I thought it must be an inside job. The average person would not have the tools to remove the twin troll from the beam. I don't mind telling you that I was delighted to hear this news. The thought of the twin troll going missing during a hurricane was excellent fodder for my book. But alas, it was not to be. Further investigation revealed that some quick-thinking person at the Houston office removed the twin troll for safe keeping as hurricane Harvey was bearing down on Texas. Suffice it to say, the twin troll is no longer in California, but currently resides in Houston, Texas. Where it will turn up in the future is anyone's guess.

BIBLIOGRAPHY

Cabanatuan, Michael. "New Bay Bridge Troll finds Home on Eastern Span." SFGATE Blog, 2014.

Correll, Timothy Corrigan and Patrick Arthur Polk. *Muffler Men*. Jackson: University Press of Mississippi, 2000.

Anziano, Tony with Andrew B. Fremier and Stephen Maller. "For Whom the Troll Dwells: A Legendary Case for Supplemental Safety Measures on the New San Francisco-Oakland Bay Bridge East Span." Recommendations for the Troll Bridge Program Oversight Committee. White Paper. Caltrans. 2013. Online.

Bruce, Matthew Hagen. Untitled typescript of the attempt to remove the troll from the old bridge. No Date.

Ellson, Michele. "Bay Bridge Troll has an Alameda twin." *The Alamedan*. Friday, November 8, 2013. Online.

Fradkin, Philip L. *Magnitude 8: Earthquakes and Life along the San Andreas Fault*. Berkeley: University of California Press, 1999.

Green, Archie. *Tin Men*. Urbana: University of Illinois Press, 2002.

Hoang, Martin. "This is the Story of the Bay Bridge Troll." *Pioneer Edition*. Vol 2. 70-75. Hayward: California State University, East Bay, 2017.

Lindow, John. *Trolls: An Unnatural History*. London: Reaktion Books LTD, 2015.

Mikesell, Stephen. *A Tale of Two Bridges: The San Francisco-Oakland Bay Bridges of 1936 and 2013*. Reno: University of Nevada Press, 2017.

Nolte, Carl. "Fantastic Horned Spirit Protects the Bay Bridge." *San Francisco Chronicle*. January 5, 1990: A6.

Peterson, Gary. *2014. Battle of the Bay: Bashing A's, Thrilling Giants, and the Earthquake World Series*. Triumph Books. Amazon Digital, 2014.

"Road Warrior." *Santa Rosa Press Democrat*. Monday, November 4, 2014. Online.

Robinson, John V. "The 'Topping Out' Traditions of the High-Steel Iron Workers." *Western Folklore*. (Fall) 60.4: 243-262, 2001.

________. *Al Zampa and the Bay Area Bridges*. Charleston South Carolina: Arcadia Publishing, 2005.

Sandsmark, Fred. "Made of Steel: Alumnus Martin Hoang brings the legendary Bay Bridge Troll back to life at Cal State East Bay." *East Bay Today*. CSU East Bay.

San Francisco Chronicle Staff. *The Quake of '89*. San Francisco: Chronicle Books, 1989.

Sherman, Sharon and Skip Armstrong. *Chainsaw Sculptor: The Art of J. Chester "Skip" Armstrong*. Jackson, Mississippi: University Press of Mississippi. 2001.

Vorderbrueggen, Lisa. "Bay Bridge Troll need not fear the scrap heap." *Contra Costa Times*. August 30, 2013. Online.

Walter, Shoshanna. "Bay Bridge Troll Faces Eviction." Bay Area edition of *The New York Times*. September 1, 2011. Online.

Winchester, Simon. *A Crack at the Edge of the World: America and the Great California Earthquake of 1906*. New York: Harper Collins, 2005.

ABOUT THE AUTHOR

John V. Robinson is an award-winning photographer and writer who is the author of eight previous books including: *Spanning the Strait: Building the Alfred Zampa Memorial Bridge* (2004), *Bridging the Tacoma Narrows* (2007), *Bay Area Iron Master Al Zampa: A Life Building Bridges* (2015), and *Carquinez Bridge 1927-2007* (2017). He holds degrees from UC Berkeley and San Francisco State University. Among his awards and fellowships are a 2006 Guggenheim Fellowship in the Field of Folklore and Popular Culture and a 2007 California Council for the Humanities recipient for his documentary photography. Robinson currently is a lecturer in English at California State University, East Bay, and Las Positas College in Livermore, California.

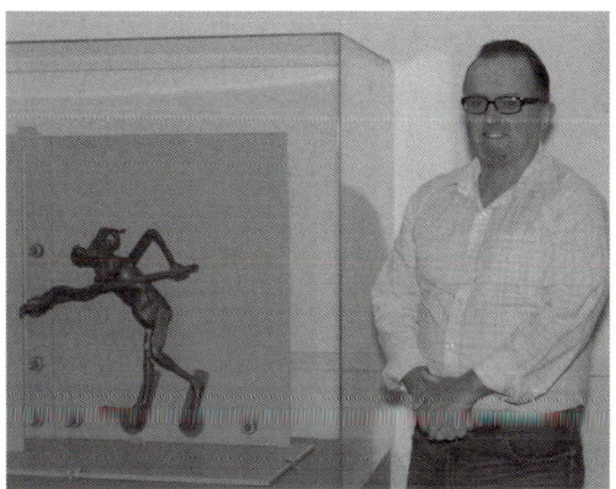

After twenty-seven years of missed connections, the author finally meets the Bay Bridge Troll, under glass, at the District 4 Caltrans office in Oakland, California. (Photo by Kyle L Ronbinson.)